ADVENT

for

EVERYONE

MATTHEW

D0822492

NEW TESTAMENT FOR EVERYONE
N. T. Wright

Matthew for Everyone, Part 1
Matthew for Everyone, Part 2
Mark for Everyone
Luke for Everyone
John for Everyone, Part 1
John for Everyone, Part 2
Acts for Everyone, Part 1
Acts for Everyone, Part 2
Paul for Everyone: Romans, Part 1
Paul for Everyone: Romans, Part 2
Paul for Everyone: 1 Corinthians
Paul for Everyone: 2 Corinthians
Paul for Everyone: Galatians and Thessalonians
Paul for Everyone: The Prison Letters
Paul for Everyone: The Pastoral Letters
Hebrews for Everyone
The Early Christian Letters for Everyone
Revelation for Everyone
Lent for Everyone: Matthew, Year A
Lent for Everyone: Mark, Year B
Lent for Everyone: Luke, Year C
Advent for Everyone: A Journey with the Apostles
Advent for Everyone: Luke
Advent for Everyone: Matthew

ADVENT
for
EVERYONE

MATTHEW

A Daily Devotional

N. T.
WRIGHT

WESTMINSTER
JOHN KNOX PRESS
LOUISVILLE · KENTUCKY

Copyright © Nicholas Thomas Wright 2016

Originally published in Great Britain in 2016 by
Society for Promoting Christian Knowledge

First published in the United States of America in 2019 by
Westminster John Knox Press

19 20 21 22 23 24 25 26 27 28—10 9 8 7 6 5 4 3 2 1

All rights reserved. No part of this book may be reproduced or transmitted
in any form or by any means, electronic or mechanical, including photo-
copying, recording, or by any information storage or retrieval system,
without permission in writing from the publisher. For information, address
Westminster John Knox Press, 100 Witherspoon Street, Louisville, Kentucky
40202-1396. Or contact us online at www.wjkbooks.com.

Scripture quotations are taken from *The New Testament for Everyone* by Tom
Wright, copyright © Nicholas Thomas Wright 2011.

Cover design by Allison Taylor

Library of Congress Cataloging-in-Publication Data
Names: Wright, N. T. (Nicholas Thomas), author.
Title: Advent for everyone : Matthew : a daily devotional / N.T. Wright.
Description: Louisville, Kentucky : Westminster John Knox Press, 2019. |
  Series: New testament for everyone | Originally published: London : SPCK,
  2016. |
Identifiers: LCCN 2019005260 (print) | LCCN 2019007230 (ebook) | ISBN
  9781611649505 (ebk.) | ISBN 9780664263416 (pbk. : alk. paper)
Subjects: LCSH: Advent--Meditations. | Advent--Biblical teaching. | Bible.
  Matthew--Meditations.
Classification: LCC BV40 (ebook) | LCC BV40 .W7534 2019 (print) | DDC
  242/.332--dc23
LC record available at https://lccn.loc.gov/2019005260

PRINTED IN THE UNITED STATES OF AMERICA

♾ The paper used in this publication meets the minimum requirements
of the American National Standard for Information Sciences—Permanence
of Paper for Printed Library Materials, ANSI Z39.48-1992

Most Westminster John Knox Press books are available at special quantity
discounts when purchased in bulk by corporations, organizations, and
special-interest groups. For more information, please e-mail SpecialSales
@wjkbooks.com.

CONTENTS

———•◆•———

CONTENTS

WEEK 1: A TIME TO WATCH

FIRST SUNDAY OF ADVENT

The Unexpected Visit: Matthew 24.36–44

[36]'Nobody knows what day or time this will happen,' Jesus went on. 'The angels in heaven don't know it, and nor does the son; only the father knows. [37]You see, the royal appearing of the son of man will be like the days of Noah.

[38]'What does that mean? Well, in those days, before the flood, they were eating and drinking, they were getting married and giving children in marriage, right up to the day when Noah went into the ark. [39]They didn't know about it until the flood came and swept them all away. That's what it'll be like at the royal appearing of the son of man.

[40]'On that day there will be two people working in the field. One will be taken, the other will be left. [41]There will be two women grinding corn in the mill. One will be taken, the other will be left.

[42]'So keep alert! You don't know what day your master will come. [43]But bear this in mind: if the householder had known what time of night the burglar was going to come, he would have stayed awake and wouldn't have let his house get broken into. [44]So you too must be ready! The son of man is coming at a time you don't expect.'

It was a fine Saturday afternoon in the heat of summer. The family, some on holiday from work, were relaxing in the house and the garden. Books and magazines were lying around the place, along with coffee mugs, newspapers and packets of biscuits. Everything had the look of the sort of cheerful untidiness that a large family can create in about an hour.

Suddenly there was a ring at the doorbell. Wondering vaguely which friend might be calling I went to answer it, dressed as I was in very casual clothes. There outside, to my horror, was a party of 30 or so well-dressed visitors. They had arranged, many months before, to come to look at the house, because of its historic associations. And neither I nor the family had remembered a thing about it.

You can imagine the next five minutes. I suggested that the visitors went into the garden for a little while ('to get a good look at the house from the outside'), and then mobilized the family to clear everything up. Within minutes everything was clean and tidy. The children retreated into bedrooms. We opened the front door again and the visit went ahead.

You can tidy a house in a few minutes, if you put your mind to it. But you can't reverse the direction of a whole life, a whole culture. By the time the ring on the doorbell happens it's too late. That's what this passage in Matthew 24 is about.

It has been applied to two different kinds of event, neither of which was what Jesus himself had in mind (though some think Matthew was already looking further ahead). We had better look at them first.

On the one hand, a great many readers have seen here a warning to Christians to be ready for the second coming of Jesus. This goes, obviously, with an interpretation of the earlier part of the chapter which sees the 'coming' of the son of man not as his vindication, his exaltation to heaven, but as his return to earth. We have been promised, in Acts 1, 1 Thessalonians 4 and many, many other passages, that one day, when God remakes the entire world, Jesus himself will take centre stage. He will 'appear' again, as Paul and John put it (e.g. Colossians 3.4; 1 John 3.2). Since nobody knows when that will be, it is vital that all Christians should be ready all the time.

On the other hand, many other readers have seen here a warning to Christians to be ready for their own death. Whatever precisely one thinks will happen immediately after death – and that's a subject devout Christians have often disagreed about – it's clearly important that we should, in principle, be ready for that great step into the unknown, whenever it is asked of us. That's one of many reasons why keeping short accounts with God, through regular worship, prayer, reading of scripture, self-examination and Christian obedience, matters as much as it does.

You can read the passage in either of these ways, or both. Often the voice of God can be heard in scripture even in ways the original writers hadn't imagined – though you need to retain, as the control, a clear sense of what they *did* mean, in case you make scripture 'prove' all kinds of things which it certainly doesn't. It is vital, therefore, to read the passage as it would have been heard by Matthew's first audience. A great national crisis was going to sweep over Jerusalem and its surrounding countryside at a date that was, to them, in the unknown future – though we now know it happened in AD 70, at the climax of the war between Rome and Judaea. Something was going to happen which would devastate lives, families, whole communities: something that was a terrible, frightening event and at the same time an event that was to be seen as 'the coming of the son of man', or the *parousia*, the 'royal appearing' of Jesus himself. And the whole passage indicates what this will be. It will be the swift and sudden sequence of events that will end with the destruction of Jerusalem and the Temple.

The point this passage makes comes in three stages:

First, nobody knows exactly when this will be, only that it will be within a generation (verse 36).

Second, life will go on as normal right up to the last minute. That's the point of the parallel with the time of Noah. Until the flood came to sweep everything away, ordinary life was carrying on with nothing unusual.

Third, it will divide families and work colleagues down the middle: 'One will be taken and one left.' This doesn't mean (as some have suggested) that one person will be 'taken' away by God in some kind of supernatural salvation, while the other is 'left' to face destruction. If anything, it's the opposite: when invading forces sweep through a town or village, they will 'take' some off to their deaths and 'leave' others untouched.

The result – and this is the point Jesus is most anxious to get across to his disciples, who by this stage must have been quite puzzled as to where it was all going – is that his followers must stay awake. They must be alert and keep watch – like people who know that surprise visitors are coming sooner or later but who don't know exactly when.

The warning was primarily directed to the situation of dire emergency in the first century, after Jesus' death and resurrection and before his words about the Temple came true. But they ring through subsequent centuries, and into our own day. We too live in turbulent and dangerous times. Who knows what will happen next week, next year? It's up to each church, and each individual Christian, to answer the question: are you ready? Are you awake? Are you keeping watch?

For Reflection or Discussion

How do you interpret this passage? How do you stand ready, as it exhorts?

WEEK 1: MONDAY

The Parable of the Weeds: Matthew 13.24–35

[24]He put another parable to them.

'The kingdom of heaven', he said, 'is like this! Once upon a time a man sowed good seed in his field. [25]While the workers were asleep, his enemy came and sowed weeds in among the wheat, and went away. [26]When the crop came up and produced corn, then the weeds appeared as well.

[27]'So the farmer's servants came to him.

'"Master," they said, "didn't you sow good seed in your field? Where have the weeds come from?"

[28]'"This is the work of an enemy," he replied.

'"So," the servants said to him, "do you want us to go and pull them up?"

[29]'"No," he replied. "If you do that you'll probably pull up the wheat as well, while you're collecting the weeds. [30]Let them both grow together until the harvest. Then, when it's time for harvest, I will give the reapers this instruction: 'First gather the weeds and tie them up in bundles to burn them, but gather the wheat into my barn.'"'

[31]He put another parable to them.

'The kingdom of heaven', he said, 'is like a grain of mustard seed, which someone took and sowed in his field. [32]It's the smallest of all the seeds, but when it grows it turns into the biggest of the shrubs. It becomes a tree, and the birds in the sky can then come and nest in its branches.'

[33]He told them another parable.

'The kingdom of heaven is like leaven,' he said, 'which a woman took and hid inside three measures of flour, until the whole thing was leavened.'

[34]Jesus said all these things to the crowds in parables. He didn't speak to them without a parable. [35]This was to fulfil what was spoken by the prophet:

> I will open my mouth in parables,
> I will tell the things that were hidden
> Since the very foundation of the world.

'Why doesn't God *do* something?'

That is perhaps the most frequent question that people ask Christian leaders and teachers – and those of some other faiths, too. Tragedies happen. Horrific accidents devastate lives and families. Tyrants and bullies force their own plans on people and crush opposition, and they seem to get away with it. And sensitive souls ask, again and again: why is God apparently silent? Why doesn't he step in and stop it?

These parables are not a direct answer to the question, and probably no direct answer can be given in this life. But they show, through the various different stories, that God's sovereign rule over the world isn't quite such a straightforward thing as people sometimes imagine.

Would people really like it if God were to rule the world directly and immediately, so that our every thought and action were weighed, and instantly judged and if necessary punished, in the scales of his absolute holiness? If the price of God stepping in and stopping a campaign of genocide were that he would also have to rebuke and restrain every other evil impulse, including those we all still know and cherish within ourselves, would we be prepared to pay that price? If we ask God to act on special occasions, do we really suppose that he could do that simply when we want him to, and then back off again for the rest of the time?

These parables are all about waiting and watching; and waiting and watching are what we all find difficult. The farmer waits for the harvest-time, watching in frustration as the weeds grow alongside the wheat. Not only the farmer, but also the birds wait for the tiny mustard seed to grow into a large shrub. The woman baking bread must wait for the leaven to spread its way through the dough until the whole loaf is mysteriously leavened. And that's what God's kingdom is like.

Jesus' followers, of course, didn't want to wait. If the kingdom was really present where Jesus was, coming to birth in what he was doing, then they wanted the whole thing at once. They weren't interested in God's timetable. They had one of their own, and expected God to conform to it.

Notice, in particular, what the servants say about the weeds. They want to go straight away into the cornfield and root out the weeds. The farmer restrains them, because life is never that simple. In their zeal to rid the field of weeds they are very likely to pull up some wheat as well.

Did Jesus, perhaps, have an eye here on the revolutionary groups of his day, only too ready to step into God's field and pull up what looked like weeds? There were many groups, including some of the Pharisees, who were eager to fight against pagans on the one hand and against compromised Jews on the other. These 'servants' may have intended to do God's will. They were longing for God to act, and were prepared to help him by acting themselves. But part of Jesus' whole campaign is to say that the true

7

kingdom of God doesn't come like that, because God himself isn't like that.

At the heart of the parable of the weeds and the wheat is the note of patience – not just the patience of the servants who have to wait and watch, but the patience of God himself. God didn't and doesn't enjoy the sight of a cornfield with weeds all over the place. But nor does he relish the thought of declaring harvest-time too soon, and destroying wheat along with weeds.

Many Jews of Jesus' time recognized this and spoke of God's compassion, delaying his judgment so that more people could be saved at the end. Jesus, followed by Paul and other early Christian writers, took the same view. Somehow Jesus wanted his followers to live with the tension of believing that the kingdom was indeed arriving in and through his own work, and that this kingdom would come, would fully arrive, not all in a bang but through a process like the slow growth of a plant or the steady leavening of a loaf.

This can sometimes seem like a cop-out today, and no doubt it did in Jesus' day as well. Saying that God is delaying his final judgment can look, outwardly, like saying that God is inactive or uncaring. But when we look at Jesus' own public career it's impossible to say that God didn't care. Here was one who was very active, deeply compassionate, battling with evil and defeating it – and still warning that the final overthrow of the enemy was yet to come.

We who live after Calvary and Easter know that God did indeed act suddenly and dramatically at that moment. When today we long for God to act, to put the world to rights, we must remind ourselves that he has already done so, and that what we are now awaiting is the full outworking of those events. We wait with patience, not like people in a dark room wondering if anyone will ever come with a lighted candle, but like people in early morning who know that the sun has arisen and are now watching for the full brightness of midday.

For Reflection or Discussion

How do you understand God's silence? How does Jesus' insistence on patience here challenge you?

WEEK 1: TUESDAY

The Beginning of the Birth Pangs: Matthew 24.1–14

[1]Jesus left the Temple and went away. As he did so, his disciples came and pointed out the Temple buildings to him. [2]'Yes,' he said, 'and you see all these things? I'm telling you the truth: not one stone will be left standing upon another. All of them will be thrown down.'

[3]As he was sitting on the Mount of Olives, his disciples came to him privately.

'Tell us,' they said, 'when will these things happen? And what will be the sign that you are going to appear as king, and that the end of the age is upon us?'

[4]'Watch out,' replied Jesus. 'Don't let anyone deceive you. [5]You see, there will be several who will come along, using my name, telling you "I'm the Messiah!" They will fool lots of people. [6]You're going to hear about wars, actual wars and rumoured ones; make sure you don't get alarmed. This has got to happen, but it doesn't mean the end is coming yet. [7]Nations will rise against one another, and kingdoms against each other. There will be famines and earthquakes here and there. [8]All this is just the start of the birth pangs.

> [9]"Then they will hand you over to be tortured, and they will kill you. You will be hated by all nations because of my name. [10]Then several will find the going too hard, and they will betray each other and hate each other. [11]Many false prophets will arise, and they will deceive plenty of people. [12]And because lawlessness will be on the increase, many will find their love growing cold. [13]But the one who lasts out to the end will be delivered. [14]And this gospel of the kingdom must be announced to the whole world, as a witness to all the nations. Then the end will come.'

We went together to see the doctor, one rainy day in the autumn. We were excited but also very apprehensive. We had a sense of going down a road we'd often heard about but had never quite believed we would travel ourselves.

He talked us gently through the whole process. Yes, the first few months were sometimes difficult. People often felt sick, especially in the morning. There were some dangers during that time but it was normally under control. Then there would come a period of quite dramatic changes, as the new little life inside the womb made its presence felt. One would need to take care, especially with diet and with strenuous activities. Then at last, as the day grew nearer, there would be all sorts of things to watch out for: high blood pressure, various potential risks for the baby. And the birth itself: well, that was something else again, and we'd talk more about it nearer the time. But our task in the meantime was to take care, be patient, and not be alarmed by some of the strange things that were going to happen.

One of the greatest biblical images for God's future is the approaching birth of a baby. It is a time of great hope and new possibility, and also, especially before modern medicine, a time of great danger and anxiety. The medical profession can describe and study each stage of pregnancy in detail. But every couple, and of course particularly every mother, has to face them personally and live through them, even though for some it is a traumatic, painful and upsetting time. The biblical writers draw freely on this well-known experience to speak of the new world that God intends to bring to birth. And one of the high-water marks of this whole biblical theme is this chapter in Matthew, and its parallels in Mark (chapter 13) and Luke (chapter 21). This, said Jesus, is just the start of the birth pangs.

It's only with images like this that one can speak of God's future. We don't have an exact description of it, and we wouldn't be able to cope with it if we did. What we have are pictures: the birth of a baby, the marriage of a king's son, a tree sprouting new leaves. God's future will be like all these, and (of course) unlike them as well.

As far as Jesus is concerned, there are two central features of God's future. On the one hand, there is his own calling and destiny; he has spoken about it often enough in the last few chapters. He has come to Jerusalem knowing that by continuing his dramatic mission of summoning Israel to repentance he will precipitate hostility, violence and his own death. And he believes that God will vindicate him after his death, by raising him from the dead.

On the other hand, there was the fate of the Jerusalem Temple. Throughout his public career Jesus had done and said things which implied that he, not the Temple, was the real centre of God's healing and restoring work. Now he had done and said things in the Temple itself which implied that the whole place was under judgment and that he had the right to pronounce that judgment. And when the disciples pointed out to him the magnificent buildings (the Temple was generally recognized as one of the most beautiful sights in the whole world) he warned them explicitly: it was all going to come crashing down.

The disciples put two and two together. The destruction of the Temple on the one hand; on the other hand, the vindication of all that Jesus has said and done. Somehow they go with each other. If Jesus has been right all along, then the Temple will have to go. But how? And when? When will the world see that Jesus really is God's Messiah?

If you were a Roman citizen, believing that Caesar was the rightful king of the world, but living at some distance from Rome itself, you would long for the day when he would pay you a state visit. Not only would you see him for yourself, but, equally importantly, all your neighbours would realize that he really was the world's lord and master.

Much of the Roman empire was Greek-speaking; and the Greek word that they would use for such a state visit, such an 'appearing' or 'presence', was *parousia*. The same word was often used to describe what happened when gods or goddesses did something dramatic – a healing miracle, say – which was thought to reveal their power and presence. And it's this word *parousia* which the disciples use in verse 3, when they ask Jesus about what's going to happen.

They speak of three things. Each is important in the long chapter that is now beginning, containing Jesus' answer to them: the destruction of the Temple, Jesus' *parousia* or 'appearance as king', and 'the end of the age'. Throughout this chapter we have to face the questions:

12

what did they mean, what did Jesus mean in answering them, what did Matthew understand by it all – and what's it got to say to us? This calls for a cool head and an attentive mind.

For the moment we can begin to glimpse what Jesus thought it was all about. The disciples wanted to see him ruling as king, with all that that would mean, including the Temple's destruction and, indeed, the ushering in of God's new age. The present age would come to its convulsive conclusion, and the new age would be born. Well, Jesus says, there will indeed be convulsions. The birth pangs of the new age will start, in the form of wars, revolutions, famines and earthquakes. Terrible times are going to come, and those who follow him will be tested severely. Many will give it all up as just too demanding.

But they shouldn't be deceived. New would-be messiahs will appear, but the vindication of Jesus himself – his royal 'presence' or 'appearing' – won't be that sort of thing, someone else coming and leading a revolt. They must hold on, keep their nerve and remain faithful. Between the present moment and the time when all will be revealed, and Jerusalem will be destroyed, the good news of the kingdom of God which Jesus came to bring will have to spread not just around Israel, as has been the case up to now (10.5–6; 15.24), but to the whole world. There is a task for them to do in the interim period.

All of this related very specifically to the time between Jesus' public career and the destruction of the Temple in AD 70. But the echoes of meaning rumble on in every successive generation of Christian discipleship. We too are called to be faithful, to hold on and not be alarmed. We too may be called to live through troubled times and to last out to the end. We too may see the destruction of cherished and beautiful symbols. Our calling then is to hold on to Jesus himself, to continue to trust him, to believe that the one who was vindicated by God in the first century will one day be vindicated before the whole world. We too are called to live with the birth pangs of God's new age, and to trust that in his good time the new world will be born.

For Reflection or Discussion

Why does Jesus use the image of birth pangs to describe God's future? What does Matthew see as the elements of this future?

WEEK 1: WEDNESDAY

The Coming of the Son of Man: Matthew 24.29–35

[29]'Straight away,' Jesus continued, 'after the suffering that those days will bring,

> The sun will turn to darkness,
> and the moon won't give its light;
> the stars will fall from heaven,
> and the powers of heaven will shake.

[30]'And then the sign of the son of man will appear in heaven; then all the tribes of the earth will mourn. They will see "the son of man coming on the clouds of heaven" with power and great glory. [31]He will send off his messengers with a great trumpet-blast, and they will collect his chosen ones from the four winds, from one end of heaven to the other.

[32]'Learn the hidden meaning from the fig tree. When its branch begins to sprout, and to push out its leaves, then you

know that summer is nearly there. [33]So with you: when you see all these things, you will know that it is near, at the very gates. [34]I'm telling you the truth: this generation won't be gone before all these things happen. [35]Heaven and earth will disappear, but my words will never, ever disappear.'

A friend of mine is a composer. (It's something I would like to have been myself, had things worked out differently, so I take a particular interest in what he does.) I watched one day as he worked on a particular piece he was writing. The large sheet of music paper sat there in front of him, with a dozen or more sets of lines waiting for notes to be written on them.

He was, at that moment, writing the clarinet part. He had already pencilled in the violins, several staves below. There were a couple of scribbles where the brass would go, somewhere in between. He had an idea about the flute and piccolo, and a few notes in their part were already there to give an indication of what would be balancing the clarinet in the woodwind section.

I left him to it and got on with other things. An hour or two later we met for coffee, and he showed me the page. It was more or less complete. In order to make about 15 seconds' worth of music, he had had to spend several hours writing out, one by one in turn, the individual line for each instrument. They would be heard all together, but they needed (of course) to be written out separately.

Now imagine that process in reverse. Listen to a short piece of music. It's over in a few seconds. But now go to the orchestra and ask the instruments to play their lines one after the other. There may well be several minutes between when the piccolo begins and when the double bass concludes. What is essentially one short piece of music could be spun out over quite some time.

Reading the sort of section now in front of us demands that sort of imagination. Often in the Bible there are passages in which several things have come rushing together into one short, tight-packed chord or musical sequence. But in order to understand them, we have to take them apart and allow them to be heard one after the other. Particularly when it comes to prophecy, the biblical writers often spoke of something which sounded as though it was all one event but which they knew might well be, and we know actually was, a sequence of events, one after the other.

The tune that this passage is playing is called 'the coming of the son of man'. In some parts of today's church, it's almost the only tune they sing, and I am concerned that they usually sing it in the wrong key. The orchestration is rich and dense. It needs looking at bit by bit.

Here's a bit from the prophet Isaiah. 'The sun will be darkened, the moon won't shine, the stars will fall from the sky, and the heavenly powers will be shaken.' What does that mean?

For Isaiah, and for those who read him in the first century, the one thing it didn't mean was something to do with the actual sun, moon and stars in the sky. That would make a quite different tune. This language was well known, regular code for talking about what we would call huge social and political convulsions. When we say that empires 'fall', or that kingdoms 'rise', we don't normally envisage any actual downward or upward physical movement. Matthew intends us to understand that the time of the coming of the son of man will be a time when the whole world seems to be in turmoil.

16

But what will this 'coming' itself actually *be*? What will Jesus' 'royal appearing' consist of? Matthew takes us back, in line with so much in Jesus' teaching, to the prophet Daniel again, and this time to the crucial passage in 7.13 (verse 30 in our present passage). They will see, he says, 'the son of man coming on the clouds of heaven'. Now in Daniel this certainly refers, not to a *downward* movement of this strange human figure, but to an *upward* movement. The son of man 'comes' from the point of view of the heavenly world, that is, he comes *from* earth *to* heaven. His 'coming' in this sense, in other words, is not his 'return' to earth after a sojourn in heaven. It is his ascension, his vindication, the thing which demonstrates that his suffering has not been in vain.

What is it, then, that will demonstrate that Jesus has been vindicated by God? Three things.

First, his resurrection and ascension. These great, dramatic, earth-shattering events will reverse the verdicts of the Jewish court and the pagan executioners. They will show that he is indeed 'the son of man' who has suffered at the hands of the 'beasts' or 'monsters' – who now, it seems, include the Temple and those who run it! – and is nevertheless then declared by God to be his true spokesman.

Second, the destruction of the Temple. Jesus, speaking as a prophet, predicted that it would fall, not as an arbitrary exercise of his prophetic powers but because the Temple had come to symbolize all that was wrong with the Israel of his day. And he had predicted the terrible suffering that would precede it. That's why, in verse 25, he underlines the fact that he has told them about it beforehand. They are to trust that he is a true prophet. They must not be deceived by the odd things that others may do to lead them astray.

And when the Temple finally falls, that will be the sign that he was speaking the truth. That will be his real vindication. His exaltation over the world, and over the Temple, will be written in large letters into the pages of history; or, as they would put it, 'they will see the sign of the son of man . . . in heaven' (verse 30).

Third, the news of his victory will spread rapidly throughout the world. What people will see is strange messengers, alone or in small groups, travelling around from country to country telling people that a recently executed Jewish prophet has been vindicated by God, that he is the Messiah and the Lord of the world. But that's just the surface event. The deeper dimension of these happenings is that the one true God is announcing to his whole creation that Jesus is his appointed Lord of the world. Or, as they would put it, 'he will send off his messengers' (or 'angels') and 'collect his chosen ones from the four winds, from one end of heaven to the other'. If we are to understand the biblical writers, we have to learn, once again, to read their language in their way.

All this is spoken to Jesus' disciples so they will know when the cataclysmic events are going to happen. Watch for the leaves on the tree, and you can tell it's nearly summer. Watch for these events, and you'll know that the great event, the destruction of the Temple and Jesus' complete vindication, is just around the corner. And be sure of this, says Jesus (and Matthew wants to underline this): it will happen within a generation.

That is an extra important reason why everything that has been said in the passage so far must be taken to refer to the destruction of Jerusalem and the events that surround it. Only when we appreciate how significant that moment was for everything Jesus had said and done will we understand what Jesus himself stood for.

But remember the composer and the music. In the long purposes of God, we who read passages like this many centuries later may find that what was said as a single statement, one short piece of music, can then be played as a string of separate parts, one after the other. I see no reason why, once we are quite clear about its original meaning, we should not then see the chapter as a pointer to other events, to the time we still await when God will complete what he began in the first century, and bring the whole created order, as Paul promised in Romans 8, to share the liberty of the glory of God's children. As we look back to the first century, we should also look on to God's still-promised future, and thank him that Jesus is already enthroned as Lord of all time and history.

For Reflection or Discussion

What do you understand by the phrase 'the coming of the son of man'? What demonstrates that Jesus has been vindicated by God?

WEEK 1: THURSDAY

The Wise and Wicked Slaves: Matthew 24.45–51

[45]'So,' Jesus went on, 'who then is the trustworthy and sensible slave, the one the master will set over his household, so that he will give them their meals at the right time? [46]Blessings on the servant whom the master, when he comes, finds doing just that. [47]I'm telling you the truth: he'll promote him to be over all his belongings. [48]But if the wicked slave says in his heart, "My master's taking his time", [49]and starts to beat the

other slaves, and to feast and drink with the drunkards, [50]the master of that slave will come on a day he doesn't expect, and at a time he doesn't know. [51]He will cut him in two, and put him along with the hypocrites, where people will weep and grind their teeth.'

The managing director was returning from a meeting out of town when he saw a familiar but unexpected sight. There, turning out of a street ahead of him, was one of his own company's vans. What was it doing here? The company didn't do business with anyone in this part of the town. What was going on?

He took the number of the van, and later in the day called the driver in. He confessed. He'd been moonlighting – working for another company at the same time, while he was supposed to be making deliveries for the company which owned the vans. He'd been, in that sense, a hypocrite, a play-actor, pretending to be one thing while in fact being another. That was his last day working for that company.

Of course, today they put electronic components into trucks and vans which record everything that happens – speed, rest periods, fuel consumption, you name it. 'The spy in the cab', the drivers call it, resentfully. But at least they know they aren't going to get away with cheating. No chance of the boss suddenly coming upon them doing something they shouldn't.

The scene changes. But the underlying drama is the same. This time we imagine a householder going away on business and coming back suddenly: will he find the workers (in that world, the slaves) doing what they should, or not? In that world a story about a master and servants would almost certainly be understood as a story about God and

Israel. God has left Israel with tasks to perform; when he comes back, what will his verdict be on how they have accomplished them?

At the same time, there may be here a further twist to this plot, from the point of view of Jesus speaking to the disciples on the Mount of Olives. He is going to leave them with work to do: the gospel must be announced to all the nations (24.14). Some of them will have responsibilities within the young and struggling Christian community. How will they discharge them?

The options presented here are stark. The slave in charge of the household has duties and must do them. If he thinks to himself that his master won't be back for a long while yet, and decides to live it up, have a good time and (for good measure) ill-treat his fellow-slaves, he will be in deep trouble. He will be a play-actor, a hypocrite. He will be pretending to be one thing while being another.

The difference between the two types of slave – the one who kept watch and did what he should, and the one who forgot what he was about and did the opposite – isn't just the difference between good and bad, between obedience and disobedience. It's the difference between wisdom and folly. This either/or is characteristic of much of Jesus' teaching in Matthew, and it's worth taking a minute to notice where it comes from.

Deep within ancient Jewish tradition we find the book of Proverbs. There, mostly in short sayings but sometimes in more extended pictures, we find in a wealth of detail the contrast between the wise person and the foolish person. Of course, ultimately the wise person is the one who respects and honours God, and the fool is the one who forgets him. But their wisdom and folly work themselves

21

out in a thousand different ways in daily life, in business, in the home and village, in making plans for the future, in how they treat other people, in their honesty or dishonesty, in their hard work or laziness, in their ability to recognize and avoid temptations to immorality. Jesus is here invoking this whole tradition of wisdom-writing, which continued to develop in Judaism after the Old Testament, and which came into early Christianity in books like the letter of James.

But now the point of 'wisdom' and 'folly' is not just being able to do what God wants in any and every situation. If the living God might knock at the door at any time, wisdom means being ready at any time. What's more, once Jesus has come, bringing God's kingdom to bear on the world, being wise or being foolish means knowing, or not knowing, what time it is in God's timetable. Wisdom consists not least, now, in realizing that the world has turned a corner with the coming of Jesus and that we must always be ready to give an account of ourselves.

Of course these warnings are held within the larger picture of the gospel, in which Jesus embodies the love of God which goes out freely to all and sundry. Of course we shall fail. Of course there will be times when we shall go to sleep on the job. Part of being a follower of Jesus is not that we always get everything right, but that, like Peter among others, we quickly discover where we are going wrong and take steps to put it right.

But along with the welcome for sinners which Jesus announces, and the ready forgiveness that is always on offer when we fail and then come to our senses, there is the hard and high call to watchfulness and loyalty. You can't use God's grace as an excuse for going slack ('God will forgive me,' said one philosopher, 'that's his job'). Even when we don't think we're being watched, we can never forget that much is expected of those to whom much is given.

For Reflection or Discussion

Does seeing this story in its Jewish context help you? How do you try to be wise in the biblical sense?

WEEK 1: FRIDAY

The Wise and Foolish Girls: Matthew 25.1–13

[1]"Then,' continued Jesus, 'the kingdom of heaven will be like ten girls who each took their own torches and went out to meet the bridegroom. [2]Five of them were silly, and five were sensible. [3]The silly ones took their torches, but didn't take oil with them. [4]The sensible ones took oil, in flasks, along with their torches.

[5]'The bridegroom took his time coming, and they all nodded off and went to sleep. [6]In the middle of the night a shout went up: "Here's the bridegroom! Come on and meet him!" [7]Then all the girls got up and trimmed the wicks of their torches.

[8]'The silly ones said to the sensible ones, "Give us some of your oil! Our torches are going out!"

[9]'But the sensible ones answered, "No! If we do that, there won't be enough for all of us together! You'd better go to the dealers and buy some for yourselves."

[10]'So off they went to buy oil. But, while they were gone, the bridegroom arrived. The ones who were ready went in with him to the wedding party, and the door was shut.

[11]'Later on the other girls came back. "Master, master!" they said, "open the door for us!"

[12]'"I'm telling you the truth," he said, "I don't know you."

[13]'So keep awake! You don't know the day or the hour.'

The guests had all arrived and were seated. The organ was playing. The bridegroom and the best man had been there half an hour in advance. The photographers were waiting. The flowers had all been beautifully arranged. The choir had practised their anthems. And the bride was nowhere to be seen.

Since I was supposed to be performing the service that day I went out of the church and round the corner on to the street. Then I saw her. Her car was stuck in traffic a few hundred yards away. Eventually she and her bridesmaids had decided to walk. They were coming down the street. I stepped out into the road, in my full clerical robes, and held up the traffic. Cars hooted their horns. People waved and shouted 'Good luck!' And we began the service a full 15 minutes late.

Every culture has its own way of celebrating a wedding – and its own risks of getting things wrong. I once knew a family where people were so afraid of a car breaking down on the way to the church that they hired a second one to drive behind the first, empty, just in case. But in different cultures the risks will be different. There are all sorts of traditional customs for what is after all one of the most important transitional moments in human life, when two people leave the security of their respective families and publicly declare that they are going to begin to live as a new, different family.

In the Middle East, to this day, there are some places where the customs at a wedding are quite similar to the ones described here. In the modern West, people don't normally get married in the middle of the night! But in that culture torchlight processions, late in the evening, are certainly known, and it seems as though the proceedings might have several stages, with the bridegroom likely to be delayed at an earlier venue before he arrives for the banquet itself, to be greeted at last by the bridesmaids.

So much for the local colour of this story, which otherwise might be confusing for people used to other customs. What else is going on here? What does this parable add to the warnings Jesus has already given about the need to be ready?

Even more obviously than the previous one, this story is rooted in the Jewish tradition of contrasting wisdom and folly – being sensible or being silly. The writer of Proverbs treats Wisdom and Folly as two women, and describes them calling out to men going by and offering them their respective lifestyles. Now, in this story, Lady Wisdom and Mistress Folly have each become five young girls, and the story invites its hearers to decide which they'd rather be. Obviously, wisdom in this case means being ready with the oil for the lamp, and folly means not thinking about it until it's too late.

It's probably wrong to try to guess what the oil in the story 'stands for' (some have suggested that it means good works, others faith, or love, or almost any of the Christian virtues). It isn't that kind of story. Within the world of the story itself, it simply means being ready for the key moment. You can't squash all these parables together and make the details fit with each other; *all* the girls in this parable, including the 'wise' ones, go to sleep in verse 5, whereas in verse 13 Jesus tells his followers to stay awake. Again, that kind of detailed question misses the point. What matters is being ready; being watchful; being wise; thinking ahead, realizing that a crisis is coming sooner or later and that if you don't make preparations now, and keep them in good shape in the meantime, you'll wish you had.

There is one other aspect to this particular story which has roots deep in the Jewish context and has given rise to a tradition of hymn-writing about the coming of the bridegroom. Already in Matthew's gospel Jesus has referred to himself as the bridegroom (9.15). In a previous parable Jesus spoke of the kingdom as being like a king making a marriage feast for his son (22.2). Mention of a bridegroom hints again at Jesus' messiahship.

This highlights the fact that the parable isn't just about the very end of time, the great and terrible day for which the world and the church still wait. Throughout his ministry, Jesus was coming as Messiah to his people, Israel. They were the ones invited to the wedding feast. They, in this story, are divided between the wise, who know Jesus and make sure they keep alert for his 'coming', and the foolish, to whom at the end Jesus will say 'I don't know you' (verse 12, echoing 7.23).

It is tempting to move away from this conclusion, because saying that parts of Jesus' teaching related particularly to a unique situation in his own time might make it look as though they are irrelevant for every other time. But that's not so. It is because what Jesus did was unique and decisive, changing for ever the way the world is and how God relates to it, that we have entered a new era in which his sovereign rule is to be brought to bear on the world. And in this new era, no less than in the unique time of Jesus and his first followers, we need as much as ever the warning that it's easy to go slack on the job, to stop paying attention to God's work and its demands, to be unprepared when the moment suddenly arrives.

For Reflection or Discussion

What, in practice, might being ready for Jesus involve in your life? And in the life of your church?

WEEK 1: SATURDAY

Gethsemane: Matthew 26.36–46

[36]So Jesus went with them to the place called Gethsemane.

'You sit here,' he said to the disciples, 'while I go over there and pray.'

[37]He took Peter and the two sons of Zebedee with him, and began to be very upset and distressed.

[38]'My soul is overwhelmed with grief,' he said, 'even to death. Stay here and keep watch with me.'

[39]Then, going a little further on, he fell on his face and prayed.

'My father,' he said, 'if it's possible – please, please let this cup go away from me! But . . . not what I want, but what you want.'

[40]He came back to the disciples and found them asleep.

'So,' he said to Peter, 'couldn't you keep watch with me for a single hour? [41]Watch and pray so that you don't get pulled down into the time of testing. The spirit is eager, but the body is weak.'

[42]Again, for the second time, he went off and said, 'My father, if it's not possible for this to pass unless I drink it, let your will be done.'

[43]Again he came and found them asleep; their eyes were heavy. [44]Once more he left them and went away. He prayed for the third time, using the same words once again. [45]Then he came back to the disciples.

'You can sleep now,' he said, 'and have a good rest! Look – the time has come, and the son of man is given over into the hands of wicked people! [46]Get up and let's be going. Look! Here comes the one who's going to betray me!'

There was once a small girl who had never seen her father anything but cheerful.

As long as she could remember, he seemed to have been smiling at her. He had smiled when she was born, the daughter he had longed for. He had smiled as he held her in his arms and helped her to learn to eat and drink. He had laughed as he played with her, encouraged her with games and toys as she learned to walk, chatted brightly as he took her to school. If she hurt herself, his smile and gentle kiss helped her to relax and get over it. If she was in difficulties or trouble, the shadow that would cross his face was like a small cloud which hardly succeeded in hiding the sun; soon the smile would come out again, the eager interest in some new project, something to distract, to move on to new worlds.

And then one day it happened.

To begin with she wasn't told why. He came back home from a visit, and with a look she'd never seen before went straight to his room. Ever afterwards she would remember the sounds she then heard, the sounds she never thought to hear.

The sound of a healthy, strapping 30-year-old man weeping for a dead sister.

It was of course a necessary part of growing up. In most families, grief would have struck sooner. Looking back, she remained grateful for the years when smiles and laughter were all she could remember. But the shock of his sudden vulnerability, far more than the fact of the death of her aunt and all that it meant, were what made the deepest impression.

I think Gethsemane was the equivalent moment for the disciples.

28

Oh, Jesus had been sad at various times. He'd been frustrated with them for not understanding what he was talking about. He'd been cross with the people who were attacking him, misunderstanding him, accusing him of all sorts of ridiculous things. There had even been tension with his own family. But basically he'd always been the strong one. Always ready with another story, another sharp one-liner to turn the tables on some probing questioner, another soaring vision of God and the kingdom. It was always they who had the problems, he who had the answers.

And now this.

Jesus was like a man in a waking nightmare. He could see, as though it was before his very eyes, the cup. Not the cup he had spoken of, and given them to drink, in the intense and exciting atmosphere of the Last Supper an hour or so before. This was the cup he had mentioned to James and John (20.22–23), the cup the prophets had spoken of. The cup of God's wrath.

He didn't want to drink it. He badly didn't want to. Jesus at this point was no hero-figure, marching boldly towards his oncoming fate. He was no Socrates, drinking the poison and telling his friends to stop crying because he was going to a much better life. He was a man, as we might say, in melt-down mode. He had looked into the darkness and seen the grinning faces of all the demons in the world looking back at him. And he begged and begged his father not to bring him to the point of going through with it. He prayed the prayer he had taught them to pray: don't let us be brought into the time of testing, the time of deepest trial!

And the answer was no.

29

Actually, we can see the answer being given, more subtly than that implies, as the first frantic and panicky prayer turns into the second and then the third. To begin with, a straight request ('Let the cup pass me by'), with a sad recognition that God has the right to say 'No' if that's the way it has to be. Then, a prayer which echoes another phrase in the Lord's Prayer: if it has to be, 'May your will be done.' The disciples probably didn't realize that, when Jesus gave them the Lord's Prayer (6.9–13), this much of it would be so directly relevant to him. He had to live what he taught. Indeed, the whole Sermon on the Mount seemed to be coming true in him, as he himself faced the suffering and sorrow of which he'd spoken, on his way to being struck on the cheek, to being cursed and responding with blessings. Here, for the second time in the gospel narrative (the first time being the temptation story in 4.1–11), we see Jesus fighting in private the spiritual battle he needed to win if he was then to stand in public and speak, and live, and die for God's kingdom.

The shocking lesson for the disciples can, of course, be turned to excellent use if we learn, in our own prayer, to wait with them, to keep awake and watch with Jesus. At any given moment, someone we know is facing darkness and horror: illness, death, bereavement, torture, catastrophe, loss. They ask us, perhaps silently, to stay with them, to watch and pray alongside them.

Distance is no object. In any one day we may be called to kneel in Gethsemane beside someone dying in a hospital in Nairobi, someone being tortured for her faith in Burma, someone who has lost a job in New York, someone else waiting anxiously for a doctor's report in Edinburgh. Once we ourselves get over the shock of realizing that all our friends, neighbours and family, and even the people we have come to rely on, are themselves vulnerable and need our support – if even Jesus longed for his friends' support, how much more should we! – we should be prepared to give it to the fullest of our ability.

And when we ourselves find the ground giving way beneath our feet, as sooner or later we shall, Gethsemane is where to go. That is where we find that the Lord of the world, the one to whom is now committed all authority (28.18), has been there before us.

For Reflection or Discussion

Does this passage shed light on how you can face the darkness and horror of life? Or on how you can help others to do the same?

WEEK 2: A TIME TO REPENT

SECOND SUNDAY OF ADVENT

The Preaching of John the Baptist: Matthew 3.1–10

[1] In those days John the Baptist appeared. He was preaching in the Judaean wilderness.

[2] 'Repent!' he was saying. 'The kingdom of heaven is coming!'

[3] John, you see, is the person spoken of by Isaiah the prophet, when he said,

> The voice of someone shouting in the desert:
> 'Prepare the route that the Lord will take,
> Straighten out his paths!'

[4] John himself had clothing made from camel's hair, and a leather belt around his waist. His food was locusts and wild honey. [5] Jerusalem, and all Judaea, and the whole area around the Jordan, were going off to him. [6] They were being baptized by him in the river Jordan, confessing their sins.

[7] He saw several Pharisees and Sadducees coming to be baptized by him.

'You brood of vipers!' he said to them. 'Who warned you to escape from the coming wrath? [8] You'd better prove your repentance by bearing the right sort of fruit! [9] And you needn't start thinking to yourselves, "We have Abraham as our father." Let me tell you, God is quite capable of raising up children for Abraham from these stones! [10] The axe is already taking aim at the root of the tree. Every tree that doesn't produce good fruit is to be cut down and thrown into the fire.'

The road, the water, the fire and the axe. Four powerful symbols set the scene for where the story of Jesus really starts.

Think first of a police motorcade sweeping through a city street. First there appear motorcycles with flashing blue lights. People scurry to the side of the road as they approach. Everybody knows what's happening: the king has been away a long time, and he's come back at last. Two large black cars come by, filled with bodyguards and officials. Then the car with a flag at the front, containing the king himself. By this time the road is clear; no other cars are in sight; everyone is standing still and watching, waving flags and celebrating.

Now take this scene back 2,000 years, and into the hot, dusty desert. The king has been away a long time, and word goes round that he's coming back at last. But how? There isn't even a road. Well, we'd better get one ready. So off goes the herald, shouting to the peoples of the desert: the king is coming! Make a road for him! Make it good and straight!

That message had echoed through the life of the Jewish people for hundreds of years by the time of John the Baptist, ever since it was first uttered in Isaiah 40. It was part of the great message of hope, of forgiveness, of healing for the nation after the horror of exile. God would at last come back, bringing comfort and rescue. Yes, John is saying; that's what's happening now. It's time to get ready! The king, God himself, is coming back! Get ready for God's kingdom! And John's striking message made everyone sit up and take notice. In today's language, they saw the blue flashing lights, and stopped what they were doing to get ready.

But the trouble was that they *weren't* ready, not by a long way. You may think your house is reasonably tidy and well kept, but if you suddenly get word that the king is coming to visit you may well suddenly want to give it another spring-clean. And the Jewish people, even the devout ones who worshipped regularly in the Temple, knew in their bones that they weren't ready for God to come back. The prophets had said that God would come back when the people repented, turning to him with all their hearts. That was what John summoned them to do; and they came in droves.

They came for baptism. John was plunging them in the water of the river Jordan as they confessed their sins. This wasn't just a symbolic cleansing for individuals; it was a sign of the new thing that God was doing in history, for Israel and the world. Over 1,000 years before, the children of Israel had crossed the Jordan when they first entered and conquered the promised land. Now they had to go through the river again, as a sign that they were getting ready for a greater conquest, God's defeat of all evil and the establishment of his kingdom on earth as in heaven.

John's message wasn't all comfort. Far from it. He spoke of a fire that would blaze, an axe that would chop down the tree. When he saw some of the Jewish religious leaders, the Pharisees and Sadducees, coming for baptism, he scoffed at them. They were like snakes slithering away from the bonfire, where they'd been hiding, as soon as it started to burn. The only thing that would make John change his mind about them would be if they really behaved differently. Going through the motions of baptism wasn't enough. Real repentance meant a complete and lasting change of heart and life. That was the only way to get the road ready for the coming king.

So what were they to repent of? The Pharisees prided themselves on their purity; they were unlikely to be guilty of gross or obvious sins. Yes, but their pride itself was getting in the way of God's homecoming, and their arrogance towards other Israelites, let alone towards the rest of the world, was quite out of keeping with the humility needed before the coming king.

In particular, John attacks their confidence in their ancestry. 'We have Abraham as our father,' they would say to themselves. In other words, 'God made promises to Abraham; we are his children; therefore God is committed to us, and we are bound to be all right in the end.' Not so fast, warns John. Your God is the sovereign creator, and it's no trouble to him to create new children for Abraham out of the very stones at your feet. The axe is ready and waiting to chop down the tree; when the king arrives, he will bring judgment as well as mercy, and the only way to avoid it is to show that you are a fruitful tree. (Jesus himself used this image on more than one occasion.) The alternative is the bonfire.

John's stark warnings set the tone for much of the story of Jesus. John prepared the way, not knowing what it would actually look like when God's kingdom arrived; and John was himself puzzled at the outcome (11.2–6). Jesus' own mission was quite different from what people sometimes imagine; the comfort and healing of his kingdom-message was balanced by the stern and solemn warning that when God comes back he demands absolute allegiance. If God really is God, he isn't simply the kindly, indulgent, easy-going parent we sometimes imagine.

The God who came to his people in Jesus will one day unveil his kingdom in all its glory, bringing justice and joy to the whole world. How can we get ready for that day? Where do the roads need straightening out? What fires need to be lit, to burn away the rubbish in his path? Which dead trees will need to be cut down? And, equally important, who should be summoned, right now, to repent?

For Reflection or Discussion

What was the situation of the Jewish people at the coming of John the Baptist? How did John say they were to get ready for Jesus?

WEEK 2: MONDAY

Jesus' Baptism: Matthew 3.11–17

[11]'I am baptizing you with water, for repentance,' John continued. 'But the one who is coming behind me is more powerful than me! I'm not even worthy to carry his sandals. He will baptize you with the holy spirit and fire! [12]He's got his shovel in his hand, ready to clear out his barn, and gather all his corn into the granary. But he'll burn up the chaff with a fire that will never go out.'

[13]Then Jesus arrived at the Jordan from Galilee, and came to John to be baptized by him.

[14]John tried to stop him.

'I ought to be baptized by you,' he said, 'And are you going to come to me?'

[15]'This is how it's got to be right now,' said Jesus. 'This is the right way for us to complete God's whole saving plan.'

So John consented, [16]and Jesus was baptized. All at once, as he came up out of the water, suddenly the heavens were opened, and he saw God's spirit coming down like a dove and landing on him.

[17]Then there came a voice out of the heavens.

'This is my son, my beloved one,' said the voice. 'I am delighted with him.'

It's safe to say that John was as surprised as we are.

Or at least, as we should be if we read this passage without knowing what's coming. To get the flavour, imagine that we are going to a huge concert hall, packed to the doors with eager and excited music-lovers. We all have our programmes in hand, waiting for the thunderous music to begin. We know what it ought to sound like. This will be music for a battle, for a victory, thunder and lightning and explosions of wonderful noise. The concert manager comes on stage and declares in ringing tones that the famous musician has arrived. He gets us all on our feet, to welcome with an ovation the man who is going to fulfil all our expectations.

As we stand there eagerly, a small figure comes on the stage. He doesn't look at all like what we expected. He is carrying, not a conductor's baton, to bring the orchestra to life, but a small flute. As we watch, shocked into silence, he plays, gently and softly, a tune quite different from what we had imagined. But, as we listen, we start to hear familiar themes played in a new way. The music is haunting and fragile, winging its way into our imaginations and hopes and transforming them. And, as it reaches its close, as though at a signal, the orchestra responds with a new version of the music we had been expecting all along.

Now listen to John as the concert manager, whipping us into excitement at the soloist who is going to appear. 'He's coming! He's more powerful than me! He will give you God's wind and God's fire, not just water! He'll sort you out – he'll clear out the mess – he'll clean up God's farm so that only the good wheat is left!' We are on our feet, expecting a great leader, perhaps the living

God himself, sweeping into the hall with a great explosion, a blaze of light and colour, transforming everything in a single blow.

And instead we get Jesus. A Jesus who comes and stands humbly before John, asking for baptism, sharing the penitential mood of the rest of Judaea, Jerusalem and Galilee. A Jesus who seems to be identifying himself, not with a God who sweeps all before him in judgment, but with the people who are themselves facing that judgment and needing to repent.

John, of course, is horrified. He seems to have known that Jesus was the one he was waiting for; but why then would he be coming for baptism? What's happened to the agenda? What's happened to the wind and fire, to the clearing out of God's farm? Surely if anything he, John, needs to be baptized by Jesus himself?

Jesus' reply tells us something vital about the whole gospel story that is going to unfold before our surprised gaze. Yes, he is coming to fulfil God's plan, the promises which God made ages ago and has never forgotten. Yes, these are promises which will blow God's wind, God's spirit, through the world, which will bring the fire of God's just judgment on evil wherever it occurs, and which will rescue God's penitent people once and for all from every kind of exile to which they have been driven. But if he, Jesus, is to do all this, this is how he must do it: by humbly identifying himself with God's people, by taking their place, sharing their penitence, living their life and ultimately dying their death.

What good will this do? And how will it bring about the result that John – and his audience – were longing for?

To those questions, Matthew's full answer is: read the rest of the story. But we can already glimpse what that answer will be when Jesus comes up out of the water. Israel came through the water of the Red Sea and was given the law, confirming their status as God's son, God's firstborn. Jesus came up from the water of baptism and received God's spirit, God's wind, God's breath, in a new way, declaring him to be God's son, Israel-in-person. The dove, though, which for a moment embodies and symbolizes the spirit, indicates that the coming judgment will not be achieved through a warlike or vindictive spirit, but will mean the making of peace. Judgment itself is judged by this spirit, just as Jesus will at last take the judgment upon himself and make an end of it.

Part of the challenge of this passage is to learn afresh to be surprised by Jesus. He comes to fulfil God's plans, not ours, and even his prophets sometimes seem to misunderstand what he's up to. He will not always play the music we expect. But if we learn to listen carefully to what he says, and watch carefully what he does, we will find that our real longings, the hunger beneath the surface excitement, will be richly met.

At the same time, those who in repentance and faith follow Jesus through baptism and along the road where he will now lead us will find, if we listen, that the same voice from heaven speaks to us as well. As we learn to put aside our own plans and submit to his, we may be granted moments of vision, glimpses of his greater reality. And at the centre of that sudden sight we will find our loving father, affirming us as his children, equipping us, too, with his spirit so that our lives may be changed, swept clean and made ready for use.

For Reflection or Discussion

What does Jesus' baptism tell you about who he is? How does it speak to you?

WEEK 2: TUESDAY

Announcing the Kingdom: Matthew 4.12–17

[12]When Jesus heard that John had been arrested, he went off to Galilee. [13]He left Nazareth, and went to live at Capernaum, a small town by the sea in the region of Zebulon and Naphtali. [14]This happened so that the word spoken through Isaiah the prophet might come true:

> [15]The land of Zebulon and the land of Naphtali,
> The road by the sea, beyond the Jordan,
> Galilee, land of the nations:
> [16]The people who sat in the dark saw a great light;
> Light dawned on those who sat in the shadowy land
> of death.

[17]From that time on Jesus began to make his proclamation. 'Repent!' he would say. 'The kingdom of heaven is arriving!'

I once knew a small boy (no, it wasn't me, actually) who used to telephone people at random. When a voice answered the phone, he would say, 'Are you on the line?' 'Yes,' the unsuspecting victim would reply. 'Well, get off quick!' he would shout. 'There's a train coming!'

The warning of an approaching object or event is always important. We need to know what's coming, what danger it poses, what action we should take. And in the case of Jesus, and of the way Matthew tells us about him, there is one thing supremely important: we need to know what this kingdom of heaven is that he said was approaching, and what action he expected people to take. Though this is central to everything Jesus was and did, and to everything that the gospels say about him, it is remarkable how few people really grasp what was going on.

First things first. Matthew normally has Jesus speak of the 'kingdom of heaven'; the other gospels normally use the phrase 'kingdom of God'. Saying 'heaven' instead of 'God' was a regular Jewish way of avoiding the word 'God' out of reverence and respect. We must clear out of our minds any thought that 'kingdom of heaven' means a place, namely 'heaven', seen as the place where God's people go after their death. That, after all, would make no sense here. How could this sort of kingdom be said to be 'approaching' or 'arriving'?

No. If 'kingdom of heaven' means the same as 'kingdom of God', then we have a much clearer idea of what Jesus had in mind. Anyone who was warning people about something that was about to happen must have known that the people he was talking to would understand. And any first-century Jew, hearing someone talking about God's kingdom, or the kingdom of heaven, would know. This meant revolution.

Jesus grew up in the shadow of kingdom-movements. The Romans had conquered his homeland about 60 years before he was born. They were the last in a long line of pagan nations to do so. They had installed Herod the Great, and then his sons after him, as puppet monarchs to do their dirty work for them. Most Jews resented both parts of this arrangement, and longed for a chance to revolt.

But they weren't just eager for freedom in the way that most subject peoples are. They wanted it because of what they believed about God, themselves and the world. If there was one God who had made the whole world, and if they were his special people, then it couldn't be God's will to have pagan foreigners ruling them. What's more, God had made promises in their scriptures that one day he would indeed rescue them and put everything right. And these promises focused on one thing in particular: God would become king. King not only of Israel but of the whole world. A king who would bring justice and peace at last, who would turn the upside-down world the right way up again. There should be no king but God, the revolutionaries believed. God's kingdom, the kingdom of heaven, was what they longed for, prayed for, worked for and were prepared to die for.

And now Jesus was declaring that God's kingdom, the sovereign rule of heaven, was approaching like an express train. Those who were standing idly by had better take note and get out of the way. God's kingdom meant danger as well as hope. If justice and peace are on the way, those who have twisted justice or disturbed peace may be in trouble. They had better get their act together while there's time. And the good old word for that is: 'Repent!'

The trouble with that word, too, is that people have often not understood it. They have thought it means 'feel bad about yourself'. It doesn't. It means 'change direction', 'turn round and go the other way' or 'stop what you're doing and do the opposite instead'. How you *feel* about it isn't the really important thing. It's what you *do* that matters.

Jesus believed that his contemporaries were going in the wrong direction. They were bent on revolution of the standard kind: military resistance to occupying forces, leading to a takeover of power. Part of the underlying theme of his temptations in the wilderness was the suggestion that he should use his own status, as God's Messiah, to launch some kind of movement that would sweep him to power, privilege and glory.

The problem with all these movements was that they were fighting darkness with darkness, and Israel was called – and Jesus was called – to bring God's *light* into the world. That's why Matthew hooks up Jesus' early preaching with the prophecy of Isaiah that spoke about people in the dark being dazzled by sudden light, a prophecy which went on to speak about the child to be born, the coming Messiah, through whom God would truly liberate Israel at last (Isaiah 9.1–7). Jesus could see that the standard kind of revolution, fighting and killing in order to put an end to . . . fighting and killing, was a nonsense. Doing it in God's name was a blasphemous nonsense.

But the trouble was that many of his contemporaries were eager to get on with the fight. His message of repentance was not, therefore, that they should feel sorry for personal and private sins (though he would of course want that as well), but that as a nation they should stop rushing towards the cliff edge of violent revolution, and instead go the other way, towards God's kingdom of light and peace and healing and forgiveness, for themselves and for the world.

What would happen if they didn't? Gradually, as Matthew's story develops, we begin to realize. If the light-bearers insist on darkness, darkness they shall have. If the peace-people insist on war, war they shall have. If the people called to bring God's love and forgiveness into the world insist on hating everyone else, hatred and all that it brings will come crashing around their ears. This won't be an arbitrary judgment or punishment; it will be what they themselves have been calling for. This is why they must repent while there's still time. The kingdom is coming, and they are standing in the way.

The message is just as urgent today, if not more so for us who live on this side of Calvary and Easter. Matthew would want to say to us that the kingdom which Jesus established through his own work, and his death and resurrection, now faces us with the same challenge. Are we working to extend God's kingdom in the world? Have we repented of our old ways, and are we moving, with Jesus, in the right direction? Or are we standing in the way?

For Reflection or Discussion

What do you understand by God's kingdom? What does the call to repentance say to you personally?

WEEK 2: WEDNESDAY

Jesus Condemns the Cities: Matthew 11.16–24

[16]"What picture shall I give you for this generation?' asked Jesus. 'It's like a bunch of children sitting in the town square, and singing songs to each other. [17]This is how it goes:

> You didn't dance when we played the flute,
> You didn't cry when we sang the dirge!

[18]"What do I mean? When John appeared, he didn't have any normal food or drink – and people said "What's got into him, then? Some demon?" [19]Then along comes the son of

man, eating and drinking normally, and people say, "Ooh, look at him – guzzling and boozing, hanging around with tax-collectors and other riff-raff." But, you know, wisdom is as wisdom does – and wisdom will be vindicated!'

²⁰Then he began to berate the towns where he'd done most of his powerful deeds, because they hadn't repented.

²¹'A curse on you, Chorazin!' he said. 'A curse on you, Bethsaida! If Tyre and Sidon had seen the kind of powerful things you saw, they would have repented long ago with hairshirts and ashes. ²²But I can tell you this: on the day of judgment Tyre and Sidon will have a better time of it than you will. ²³And what about you, Capernaum? You think you're going to be exalted to heaven, do you? No – you'll be sent down to Hades! If the powerful works that happened in you had happened in Sodom, it would still be standing today. ²⁴But I can tell you this: on the day of judgment the land of Sodom will have a better time of it than you will!'

A bright red sports car swept by me in the street, with a roar of exhaust and a swish of tyres. As it slowed momentarily to take the corner, I caught a glimpse of the young man driving it: dark glasses, long hair, the hint of a beard. Rock music was playing at full blast on the car's stereo. The sticker in the back window of the car said: 'I'M THE ONE YOUR MOTHER WARNED YOU ABOUT.' He was clearly proud of the fact.

Most societies have warned children about certain types of people, and the ancient Israelites were no exception. In the book called Deuteronomy, which sets out the commands and warnings given by Moses to the children of Israel immediately before they crossed the river to take possession of the promised land, there are clear warnings about certain types of persons and what they may do.

Beware of false prophets, said Moses; they will try to lead you astray from following YHWH, and you must resist them. Beware of a rebellious son, he said, one who refuses to obey his parents. He will bring evil upon Israel, and his parents must bring him to the elders of the town and have them put him to death.

This harsh commandment (Deuteronomy 21.18–21) instructs the parents of such a son to accuse him in a particular way. 'This son of ours', they must say, 'is stubborn and rebellious. He will not obey us. He is a glutton and a drunkard.' Then the people must stone him to death.

But where have we heard this sort of thing before?

In this passage – on the lips of Jesus himself. This, it seems, is what people are saying about him: he's a guzzler and a boozer, a glutton and a drunkard, he likes his parties and his food and drink. *He must be a rebellious son, leading Israel astray!* Maybe he's a false prophet as well. This charge surfaces again later in the book.

Jesus was up against it and clearly found it frustrating. John the Baptist had led a life of self-denial, like the holy ascetics in many traditions. Ordinary people had found that hard to take. They had even suspected that a demon might have got into him. Now here was Jesus himself, celebrating the kingdom of heaven with all and sundry, throwing parties which spoke of God's lavish, generous love and forgiveness – and people accused him of being a rebel, a son who wouldn't behave, a false prophet! The answer, of course, then as now, is that people don't like the challenge, either of someone who points them to a different sort of life entirely, or of someone who shows that God's love is breaking into the world in a new way, like a fresh breeze blowing through a garden and shaking old blossom off the trees.

And they certainly didn't like it when this meant Jesus challenging them to turn away from the direction they'd been going and take the opposite path instead. Some of Jesus' sternest warnings are reserved, as in verses 20–24, for those who refuse this call. Why? What was going on? Was he just angry, and calling down a curse on them?

No. These warnings are among the most sober and serious words he ever said. He had lived in Capernaum, after all; he knew the people. They were his friends, his neighbours. The baker where he bought his bread. The people he met in the synagogue. And he knew Chorazin and Bethsaida, just a short walk along the lakeside. And he knew now, despite all the remarkable things he'd done there, that they were bent on going their own way, following their own vision of God's kingdom. And he knew where that would lead.

Their vision of the kingdom was all about revolution. Swords, spears, surprise attacks; some hurt, some killed, winning in the end. Violence to defeat violence. A holy war against the unholy warriors. Love your neighbour, hate your enemy; if he slaps you on the cheek, or makes you walk a mile with him, stab him with his own dagger. That's the sort of kingdom-vision they had. And Jesus could see, with the clarity both of the prophet and of sheer common sense, where it would lead. Better be in Sodom and Gomorrah, with fire and brimstone raining from heaven, than fighting God's battles with the devil's weapons.

He was offering a last chance to embrace a different kingdom-vision. He'd outlined it in his great sermon and the teaching he was giving in towns and villages all over Galilee. He was living it out on the street, and in houses filled with laughter and friendship. He was showing how powerful it was with his healings. And they didn't want it – and were ready to use any excuse ('He's got a demon!' 'He's a guzzler and boozer!' 'He's the one they warned us about!') to avoid the issue.

For Reflection or Discussion

What are the excuses people use today to avoid the issue of the kingdom? How can you help them to see that they need to repent and change direction?

WEEK 2: THURSDAY

The Parable of Clean and Unclean: Matthew 15.10–20

[10]Then Jesus called the crowd, and said to them, 'Listen and understand. [11]What makes someone unclean isn't what goes into the mouth. It's what comes out of the mouth that makes someone unclean.'

[12]Then the disciples came to Jesus.

'Do you know', they said, 'that the Pharisees were horrified when they heard what you said?'

[13]'Every plant that my heavenly father hasn't planted', replied Jesus, 'will be plucked up by the roots. [14]Let them be. They are blind guides. But if one blind person guides another, both of them will fall into a pit.'

[15]Peter spoke up. 'Explain the riddle to us,' he said.

[16]'Are you still slow on the uptake as well?' replied Jesus. [17]'Don't you understand that whatever goes into the mouth travels on into the stomach and goes out into the toilet? [18]But what comes out of the mouth begins in the heart, and that's

what makes someone unclean. [19]Out of the heart, you see, come evil plots, murder, adultery, fornication, theft, false witness, and blasphemy. [20]These are the things that make someone unclean. But eating with unwashed hands doesn't make a person unclean.'

One of the best-loved characters in children's stories is Winnie-the-Pooh. In one escapade of this down-to-earth, loveable toy bear (the creation of the writer A. A. Milne), Pooh attempts to trap an elephant – or, as he mispronounces it, a Heffalump.

Pooh digs a hole to catch the Heffalump and decides to bait the trap with some of his own favourite food: honey. But, fond as he is of honey, he can't bear to leave a whole jar of it in the trap, and so begins to eat some himself . . . excusing himself with the thought that it's important to make sure it really *is* honey, all the way down. It wouldn't do to have anything else at the bottom. And of course, by the time he's quite sure it really *was* honey all the way down, the jar is empty . . .

For Pooh what matters is what the jar really contains, all the way down. If it's only got honey at the top, but something quite different underneath, one needs to know. And that lies at the heart of what Jesus now says, by way of comment on the earlier discussion with the Pharisees about the purity laws.

What's the point of keeping all the purity laws? In order to be the sort of person God always had in mind. What sort of person did God always have in mind? One who was pure, not just on the surface but right the way down, down to the very depths of the personality. There wasn't anything wrong with the purity laws themselves, though some of the developed traditions about them may have been fairly pointless. But to stick just with the outward laws, and ignore the call to be pure through and through, was to miss the point entirely.

Jesus' way of putting this was a riddle that must have seemed puzzling and, as this passage says, shocking to his hearers. 'It isn't what goes into the mouth, but what comes out of the mouth, that makes you unclean.' What can he mean? He surely can't be thinking of vomit, or spittle?

He is thinking of words. His point is that words reveal what the person contains, deep down. Long before psychologists noticed that what people say is an indication of what's really going on inside their thoughts and imaginations, particularly when they're not concentrating very hard, Jesus had made the same point. The actions which make someone unclean, unfit for God's holy presence, are things like murder, adultery, fornication and the rest. The motivations which point towards such actions give themselves away in thoughts and words which come bubbling up from the depths of the personality. And those thoughts and words show that, whatever outward purity codes people may keep, they still need to change inside, to repent deep down in their innermost selves, if they are to be what God intended and wanted.

So this discussion isn't simply about whether Jesus and his followers keep the traditions that the Pharisees maintained and tried to urge on other Jews. The discussion is about what God really wants his people to be like, and how this desire can be fulfilled. Here and elsewhere Jesus is addressing the deep question, which to be sure many of his contemporaries, including many of the Pharisees themselves, were well aware of: how can the human heart be made pure?

Anyone who doesn't see this as a problem – including anyone who supposes that the answer can lie simply in a list of regulations – has not yet seen the depth of wickedness that lurks inside the personality. Most of us are quite capable of most of the things listed in verse 19, and many others besides. If that's what's in our hearts, we are impure in God's eyes and need to be made clean, clean all the way down.

The point of what Jesus is saying, then, is that through his work God is offering a cure for this deep-level impurity. And this cure cuts across what other teachers of his day were offering. They saw the purity laws as the right place to start, and some of them were content to stop there too. Jesus saw these laws as largely irrelevant to the real task he had come to undertake. He was (as he said in several of the parables) sowing the seeds of the kingdom, planting plants that would grow and flourish. But people with other agendas were planting plants that would be torn up. People who were pushing the purity laws as the solution to the problems of Israel were, he said, like one blind person trying to show another blind person the way to go. Not only would both of them get lost, but both of them might well fall into a hole in the ground.

The real challenge of this passage, then, comes to all of us, especially if we think of ourselves as followers of Jesus. We may not observe the purity codes of ancient Israel, but are our hearts, our thoughts and intentions, and the casual words we utter, telling us that our own purity is less than complete?

For Reflection or Discussion

What are you doing about your own impurity? How are you going to change?

WEEK 2: FRIDAY

The Parable of the Wedding Feast: Matthew 22.1–14

[1]Jesus spoke to them once again in parables.

[2]'The kingdom of heaven', he said, 'is like a king who made a wedding feast for his son. [3]He sent his slaves to call the invited guests to the wedding, and they didn't want to come.

[4]'Again he sent other slaves, with these instructions: "Say to the guests, Look! I've got my dinner ready; my bulls and fatted calves have been killed; everything is prepared. Come to the wedding!"

[5]'But they didn't take any notice. They went off, one to his own farm, another to see to his business. [6]The others laid hands on his slaves, abused them and killed them. [7](The king was angry, and sent his soldiers to destroy those murderers and burn down their city.) [8]Then he said to his slaves, "The wedding is ready, but the guests didn't deserve it. [9]So go to the roads leading out of town, and invite everyone you find to the wedding." [10]The slaves went off into the streets and rounded up everyone they found, bad and good alike. And the wedding was filled with partygoers.

[11]'But when the king came in to look at the guests, he saw there a man who wasn't wearing a wedding suit.

[12]'"My friend," he said to him, "how did you get in here without a wedding suit?" And he was speechless. [13]Then the king said to the servants, "Tie him up, hands and feet, and throw him into the darkness outside, where people weep and grind their teeth."

[14]'Many are called, you see, but few are chosen.'

'The trouble with politicians today,' my friend said to me the other evening, 'is that they always tell us that if we vote for them things will get better. If only they'd tell us the truth – that the world is a dangerous place, that there are lots of wicked people trying to exploit each other, and that they will do their best to steer us through – then we might believe them.'

'Yes,' another friend chipped in, 'and that's what happens in the church as well. We are so eager to tell people that God loves them, that everything's going to be all right, that God welcomes wicked people as well as good ones – and then ordinary Christians have to live in the real world where people lie and cheat and grab what they want. Somehow it doesn't fit.'

I thought about this conversation again as I read this parable, which often bothers people because it doesn't say what we want it to. We want to hear a nice story about God throwing the party open to everyone. We want (as people now fashionably say) to be 'inclusive', to let everyone in. We don't want to know about judgment on the wicked, or about demanding standards of holiness, or about weeping and gnashing of teeth. Doesn't the Bible say that God will wipe away every tear from every eye?

Well, yes, it does, but you have to see that saying in its proper setting (Revelation 21.4, quoting Isaiah 25.8) to understand it. It doesn't mean that God will act like a soothing parent settling a child back to sleep after a nightmare. God wants us to be grown up, not babies, and part of being grown up is that we learn that actions have consequences, that moral choices matter, and that real human life isn't like a game of chess where even if we do badly the pieces get put back in the box at the end of the day and we can start again tomorrow. The great, deep mystery of God's forgiveness isn't the same as saying that whatever we do isn't really important because it'll all work out somehow.

This is not a lesson we want to learn. Often people dislike this parable because it teaches it.

Of course, when Jesus told the parable it had a particular point and focus. The parable follows straight on from the devastating story of the wicked tenant farmers in chapter 21, and rams the point home. Everyone would know what a story about a landowner with a vineyard was referring to; equally, everyone in Jesus' day would know the point of a story about a king throwing a wedding party for his son. This story is about the coming of God's kingdom, and in particular the arrival of the Messiah.

Israel's leaders in Jesus' day, and the many people who followed them, were like guests invited to a wedding – God's wedding party, the party he was throwing for his son. But they had refused. Galilee had refused, for the most part. Now Jerusalem was refusing the invitation as well. God was planning the great party for which they had waited so long. The Messiah was here, and they didn't want to know. They abused and killed the prophets who had tried to tell them about it, and the result was that their city would be destroyed.

But now for the good news – though it wasn't good news for the people who were originally invited. God was sending out new messengers, to the wrong parts of town, to tell everyone and anyone to come to the party. And they came in droves. We don't have to look far in Matthew's gospel to see who they were. The tax-collectors, the prostitutes, the riff-raff, the nobodies, the blind and lame, the people who thought they'd been forgotten. They were thrilled that God's message was for them after all.

But there was a difference between this wide-open invitation and the message so many want to hear today. We want to hear that everyone is all right exactly as they are; that God loves us as we are and doesn't want us to change. People often say this when they want to justify particular types of behaviour, but the argument doesn't work. When the blind and lame came to Jesus, he didn't say, 'You're all right as you are.' He healed them. They wouldn't have been satisfied with anything less. When the prostitutes and extortioners came to Jesus (or, for that matter, to John the Baptist), he didn't say, 'You're all right as you are.' His love reached them *where* they were, but his love refused to let them stay *as* they were. Love wants the best for the beloved. Their lives were transformed, healed, changed.

Actually, nobody really believes that God wants *everyone* to stay exactly as they are. God loves serial killers and child-molesters; God loves ruthless and arrogant business-men; God loves manipulative mothers who damage their children's emotions for life. But the point of God's love is that he wants them to change – to repent! He hates what they're doing and the effect it has on everyone else – and on themselves, too. Ultimately, if he's a good God, he cannot allow that sort of behaviour, and that sort of person, if he or she doesn't repent, to remain for ever in the party he's throwing for his son.

That is the point of the end of the story, which is otherwise very puzzling. Of course, within the story itself it sounds quite arbitrary. Where did all these other guests get their wedding costumes from? If the servants just herded them in, how did they have time to change their clothes? Why should this one man be thrown out because he didn't have the right thing to wear? Isn't that just the sort of social exclusion that the gospel rejects?

Well, yes, of course, at that level. But that's not how parables work. The point of the story is that Jesus is telling the truth, the truth that political and religious leaders often like to hide: the truth that God's kingdom is a kingdom in which love and justice and truth and mercy and holiness reign unhindered. They are the clothes you need to wear for the wedding. And if you refuse to put them on, if you don't feel any need to repent, you are saying you don't want to stay at the party.

For Reflection or Discussion

What does God's tough love mean for you? And for the people around you?

WEEK 2: SATURDAY

Peter's Denial: Matthew 26.69–75

⁶⁹Meanwhile, Peter sat outside in the courtyard.

One of the servant-girls came up to him. 'You were with Jesus the Galilean too, weren't you?' she said.

⁷⁰He denied it in front of everyone.

'I don't know what you're talking about,' he said.

⁷¹He went out to the gateway. Another girl saw him, and said to the people who were there, 'This fellow was with Jesus the Nazarene!'

⁷²Once more he denied it, this time swearing, 'I don't know the man!'

⁷³After a little while the people standing around came up and said to Peter, 'You really are one of them! Look – the way you talk makes it obvious!'

⁷⁴Then he began to curse and swear, 'I don't know the man!' And then, all at once, the cock crowed.

⁷⁵And Peter remembered.

He remembered the words Jesus had spoken to him: 'Before the cock crows, you will deny me three times.'

And he went outside and cried like a baby.

In his novel *Thinks* . . . , the English writer David Lodge tells the story of a woman who discovers, after his death, that her husband, whom she had loved and trusted, had been regularly unfaithful to her for several years. At the same time, she meets an unscrupulous computer scientist, who tries to persuade her, among other things, that computers can, in principle, do the things that humans can do, including thinking for themselves. She resists this idea, but with difficulty and without total conviction.

Meanwhile, she has built up a deep anger and resentment against her late husband. Finally, returning to her old home towards the end of the book, and seeing his photographs, something in her gives way; and she breaks down and cries and cries. And she forgives him.

And then she realizes the answer to the other question: this is something a computer could never, ever do. 'Crying', she says, 'is a puzzler.' It seems to come from somewhere which works closely in harmony with the bits of us that computers can replicate, and yet it goes so far beyond what they can do that we have to see tears as a key signpost of what it means to be a human being.

Peter's tears at the end of this story are the main thing that distinguish him from Judas in the next chapter. There is all the difference in the world between genuine repent-ance and mere remorse, as Paul wryly notes in one of his letters to Corinth (2 Corinthians 7.10). The one leads to life, the other to death. Peter's tears, shaming, humiliating and devastating though they were, were a sign of life. Judas's anger and bitterness led straight to death.

They had been a long time coming. Peter had recovered quite quickly, we may imagine, from the near-humiliation of trying to walk on the water only to need rescuing (14.28–31). He had, no doubt, been hurt and humiliated when Jesus spun round and told him off, telling him he was a satan (16.23). He had been perplexed with the rest of them as Jesus had done dramatic things in Jerusalem and then had failed (as it must have seemed) to capitalize on them, continuing instead with his apparent determination to walk straight into a trap. Peter had done his best in the garden, as he said he would; but his best hadn't been good enough, and he must have had a sense that he'd let Jesus down both by not defending him and in another way by trying to do so in the wrong way.

And now this. Tired, frightened, short on sleep but long on wine from the meal earlier. Doing the right thing (following Jesus) for the wrong reason (wounded pride). Or perhaps, depending how you look at it, the wrong thing (walking straight into a trap, despite Jesus warning them against the time of trial) for the right reason (dogged loyalty). Who knows, or cares? The muddled motives and mixed emotions were no match for the three little ques-tions, from a couple of serving-girls and a courtier with an ear for a northern accent. They were like small pins stuck into a large balloon, and Peter's world exploded in a roar of oaths and a flood of bitter tears.

Denying Jesus is such a sad thing to do. And yet we all do it. Despite the differences of culture and situation, we can even notice parallels, so close as to be almost amusing, between where Peter was that night and where we may find ourselves.

A good dinner, plenty of wine. Lots of excitement. Short on sleep but determined to stay in the action. Then a few questions from people we don't even know.

'You're not one of those Jesus-freaks, are you?'

'I mean, nobody here actually *believes* in Jesus, do they?'

'Well, it's all right to be interested in Jesus, but you don't want to take it to extremes, do you?'

Or perhaps it's more subtle. Where frontal attack fails, the enemy will sneak round to an unlocked side entrance.

'If I don't make it in tomorrow, you will sign the office list for me to say I was there, won't you?'

'Go on – it's just this once and nobody will know.'

'You don't mind making a little bit on the side, do you?'

It speaks volumes both for the accuracy of the gospels and for the humility of the leaders in the early church that Peter's story, in all its graphic detail, remains there starkly in all four gospels. Of course, it makes other points as well: notably, that Jesus, who told him he'd do it, was a true prophet despite what Caiaphas and the others thought. But probably the main reason for this story being told and retold was simply that it provided such an excellent example of how not to do it. The early church was full of people who started off enthusiastically and then ran the risk of losing steam halfway down the line. Today's church faces the same problem.

Equally, the early church saw many people, both great leaders and insignificant serving-girls (not that anyone is insignificant in God's family), stand up to questioning, persecution, torture and death rather than deny Jesus. If Peter could have seen young and innocent Christians, 200 years later, facing lions in the amphitheatre rather than deny their Lord, he would perhaps have felt that his negative example had served some purpose. What would he think if he could see the church today?

Like Peter, every one of us stands in daily need of the grace of God that follows true repentance, enabling us to put the past behind us, make a fresh start and continue in his service.

For Reflection or Discussion

What are the ways in which you have denied Jesus? How can you put things right?

WEEK 3: A TIME TO HEAL

THIRD SUNDAY OF ADVENT

Jesus and John the Baptist: Matthew 11.1–11

¹So when Jesus had finished giving instructions to the twelve disciples, he moved on from there to teach and preach in their towns.

²Meanwhile, John, who was in prison, heard about these messianic goings-on. He sent word through his followers.

³'Are you the one who is coming?' he asked. 'Or should we be looking for someone else?'

⁴'Go and tell John', replied Jesus, 'what you've seen and heard. ⁵Blind people are seeing! Lame people are walking! People with virulent skin diseases are being cleansed! Deaf people can hear again! The dead are being raised to life! And – the poor are hearing the good news! ⁶And God bless you if you're not upset by what I'm doing.'

⁷As the messengers were going away, Jesus began to speak to the crowds about John.

'What were you expecting to see,' he asked, 'when you went out into the desert? A reed wobbling in the wind? ⁸No? Well, then, what were you expecting to see? Someone dressed in silks and satins? If you want to see people like that you'd have to go to somebody's royal palace. ⁹All right, so what *were* you expecting to see? A prophet? Ah, now we're getting there: yes indeed, and much more than a prophet! ¹⁰This is the one the Bible was talking about when it says,

See, I'm sending my messenger ahead of you
And he will clear your path before you.

¹¹'I'm telling you the truth: John the Baptist is the greatest mother's son there ever was. But even the least significant person in heaven's kingdom is greater than he is.

We had rehearsed the show for weeks, and reckoned we had it pretty well sorted out. We were a bunch of enthusiastic amateurs, but we were quite pleased with our singing, acting and dancing. The show was going to be good, funny and exciting. People would love it. And they did.

But in the last performance, the star of the show had a new idea. He didn't tell anyone. He simply, at a crucial moment, did the opposite of what we'd rehearsed. He had realized we were in danger of getting stale, and knew that if he shocked us on stage our reactions would be all the better. He was right. We all jumped like startled rabbits, just as if we'd been practising the move for ages. The audience loved it. We all responded, and the performance became electric. It wasn't what we'd expected, but it was better than we'd dared to hope.

Throughout this chapter Jesus is dealing with the fact that what he's doing is not what people were expecting him to do. He knows it, is facing it and believes that this is the way to go, the way to bring in God's kingdom even though this isn't what others had imagined. The trouble is, though, that in terms of the illustration the other actors aren't necessarily getting the message, and the audience is getting puzzled. Later in the chapter, we'll see how the people in his own town of Capernaum were getting the wrong idea and refusing to go along with his new interpretation of what God's kingdom would be like. But we begin with something that must have been even harder for Jesus to bear. His own cousin and colleague was having doubts. Had Jesus forgotten the script? Hadn't he remembered what he was supposed to be doing?

John, we recall, was in prison; Matthew has already mentioned this (4.12) and will tell the story more fully in 14.3–12. King Herod had taken exception to John's fiery preaching, and particularly to his denunciation of him for marrying his brother's ex-wife. This was all part of John's announcement that God's kingdom – and God's true king – were on the way. Herod wasn't the real king; God would replace him. No wonder Herod put him in prison.

But now, in prison, John was disappointed. He heard about what Jesus was doing, and it didn't sound at all like the show he thought they'd rehearsed. He was expecting Jesus to be a man of fire, an Elijah-like character who would sweep through Israel as Elijah had dealt with the prophets of Baal (the pagan god many Israelites worshipped instead of YHWH). No doubt John looked forward eagerly to the day, not long now, when Jesus would confront Herod himself, topple him from his throne, become king in his place – and get his cousin out of prison and give him a place of honour.

But it seemed as though Jesus was working to a different script altogether. (Matthew refers to what Jesus was doing as 'his messianic deeds', but part of the point is that John didn't see them like that.) Jesus was going around befriending tax-collectors and 'sinners' (people whom strict Jews would regard as outsiders, not keeping the Torah properly). He was gaining a great reputation – but not for doing what John wanted him to do. What was going on? Had John been mistaken? Was Jesus after all 'the one who was to come' – the one the play demanded, the one written into the script John thought they were acting out?

Yes and no. Jesus believed – and Matthew wants us to get this clear – that he really was 'the one who was to come'. He really was the Messiah. But he had rewritten the key bit of the play, to the surprise and consternation of the other actors and the audience as well. He was going back to a different script, a different kind of story.

He wasn't thinking of himself in terms of Elijah calling down fire from heaven. He was thinking of passages like Isaiah 35, the great prophecies of what would happen when Israel was not so much judged and condemned, but restored *after* judgment. Exile would be over, the blind and the lame would be healed, God's people would be set free at last.

Jesus is actually one jump ahead, in the story-line, of where John thinks he should be. John wants him to bring judgment – and so, in a sense, he will. But already the mercy which comes after judgment, the healing which comes after the time of sorrow, is breaking in, and it's Jesus' job to bring it. This, according to Jesus (and Matthew), is the Messiah's main task.

Actually, Jesus wasn't the only one at the time who thought the Messiah would do things like this. In one of the Dead Sea Scrolls found at Qumran there's a passage which predicts that when the Messiah comes he will heal the sick, raise the dead, bring good news to the poor, and so on. The difference is that Jesus was actually *doing* these things. Just as wicked people don't like the message of judgment, because they think (rightly) that it's aimed at them, so sometimes good people don't like the message of mercy, because they think (wrongly) that people are going to get away with wickedness.

But mercy was at the heart of Jesus' messianic mission, just as it remains at the heart of the church's work today.

Whether or not that's the script people want us to follow, that's the way we've got to go. And Jesus invokes a special blessing on people who realize that this is the true story – which turns into a coded warning to those who are puzzled, including poor John himself. This is where and how God is at work. Those who recognize it, and are not offended because they were expecting something else, will know God's blessing.

For Reflection or Discussion

How can you show God's mercy? What can the church do to show mercy to the world?

WEEK 3: MONDAY

On Following Jesus: Matthew 8.14–22

[14]Jesus went into Peter's house. There he saw Peter's mother-in-law laid low with a fever. [15]He touched her hand. The fever left her, and she got up and waited on him.

[16]When evening came, they brought to him many people who were possessed by demons. He cast out the spirits with a word of command, and healed everyone who was sick. [17]This happened so that the word spoken by Isaiah the prophet might come true:

He himself took our weaknesses
And bore our diseases.

[18]When Jesus saw the crowd all around him, he told them to go across to the other side of the lake. [19]A scribe came up and spoke to him.

'Teacher,' he said, 'I will follow you wherever you go!'

²⁰Foxes have their dens,' replied Jesus, 'and the birds in the sky have their nests. But the son of man has nowhere he can lay his head.'

²¹'Master,' said another of his disciples, 'let me first go and see to my father's funeral.'

²²Follow me!' replied Jesus. 'And leave the dead to bury their own dead.'

What do you *always* do first thing in the morning?

For some, it will be shaving. For others, it will be making a cup of tea. For some, it will be vigorous exercise. For others, it will be reading the newspaper. Put it the other way: if someone forcibly prevented you from going through your normal morning routine, what would you miss most?

Now imagine what it would take, other than physical violence, to make you suddenly do everything differently. With most of us, it would be very bad news: an accident, a sudden illness or death in the family. If I received, early in the morning, a telephone call to say that a close family member had just been involved in a major accident, I wouldn't do any of my normal morning things. I would pull on whatever clothes I could grab and go to be with him or her as fast as I could.

For a devout Jew, in Jesus' day and in our own, one of the most solemn and sacred parts of the morning routine would be to say the basic Jewish prayer: 'Hear, O Israel, the Lord our God is the only Lord; and you shall love the Lord your God with all your heart . . .' It is a beautiful and haunting prayer, which has become woven into the very lifeblood of Jewish people for thousands of years. Saying this prayer is regarded by official Jewish teaching as the most important thing to do each day.

But there is one thing which takes precedence even over saying this prayer. According to the rabbis' teaching, when a man's father dies he has such a strong obligation to give him a proper burial that this comes first, before everything else – even before saying the 'Hear, O Israel' prayer.

So when Jesus found one of his followers saying that he had to go and organize his father's funeral, you'd have expected him to say, 'Oh well, of course, you must go and do that – and then come and follow me later.' What Jesus actually said is one of the most shocking things in the whole gospel story. 'Let the dead bury the dead,' he said: 'you must follow me right now.'

Of course, we don't know if the man's father had actually died yet. He may just have been getting older, perhaps becoming sick. The man may have been using his future obligation as a way of postponing following Jesus for some time, possibly for several years. He was, we may suppose, keeping his options open. But when the saying was remembered it rang like a warning bell through the Jewish hearts and minds of Jesus' hearers. What Jesus was doing was so important, so urgent, so immediate that it was the one thing that mattered. Whatever else you were thinking of doing, this comes first.

Jesus' sovereign authority sweeps on through this story like a fresh wind coming through the window and turning all the papers upside down. He heals Peter's mother-in-law; he then heals everyone who is brought to the house. But in this sequence we start to see, as well, a more rounded view of this authority. Jesus doesn't have, as it were, absolute power for its own sake. He has authority *in order to be the healer*. And he is the healer by taking the sickness and pain of all the world on to himself. In verse 17 Matthew quotes from Isaiah 53.4, a passage more often associated in Christian thinking with the meaning of Jesus' death, bearing our griefs and sorrows on the cross; but for Matthew there is no sharp line between the healing Jesus offered during his life and the healing for sin and death which he offered through his own suffering. The one leads naturally into the other.

That is why Jesus issues a solemn warning to the enthusiastic disciple who proclaims that he will follow him wherever he goes. Do you really know, he says, what you're letting yourself in for? This isn't just an exciting and triumphant march, following the one who has God's authority, watching him do mighty and powerful things all over the place. This is a commitment to one whose authority is given in order that he can go to the places where the world is in its deepest pain, and be there with and for the people who are suffering it. Even foxes and birds have places to which they can go back when they're tired. Jesus will have none. He has a temporary home in Capernaum; but now he belongs on the road, in the countryside, in the streets and lanes, wherever God's people are in need. He will have no place to rest his head until at last it rests, lifeless, on the cross.

'The son of man', he said, 'has nowhere to lay his head.' By itself the phrase 'the son of man' here is very cryptic; it could simply mean 'I' or 'someone like me'. But for Matthew, who knows several other sayings in which this strange phrase occurs, there is no question: it carries the note of authority (see e.g. 9.6; 26.64). But it also speaks of suffering (20.28). Somehow, in Matthew's picture of Jesus, we find all this rolled together: authority *through* healing, healing *through* suffering. Authority and suffering are strangely concentrated in this one man, who nobody at this stage quite understood, but who everybody found compelling. Perhaps that's the greatest challenge facing the church today: how to live the life of Jesus, how to be his followers, in such a way that people will want to follow him too.

For Reflection or Discussion

What demands does Jesus make on his followers? What is the link between Jesus' authority and his healing?

WEEK 3: TUESDAY

The Healing of the Paralytic: Matthew 9.1–8

[1]Jesus got into the boat, and crossed back over to his own town.

[2]Some people brought to him a paralysed man lying on a bed. When Jesus saw their faith, he said to the paralysed man,

'Cheer up, my son! Your sins are forgiven!'

[3]'This fellow's blaspheming!' said some of the scribes to themselves.

[4]Jesus read their thoughts. 'Why let all this wickedness fester in your hearts?' he said. [5]'Which is easier: to say "Your sins are forgiven", or to say, "Get up and walk?" [6]But, to let you know that the son of man has authority on earth to forgive sins' – he spoke to the paralysed man – 'Get up, pick up your bed, and go home!'

[7]And he got up, and went away to his home. [8]When the crowds saw it they were frightened, and praised God for giving authority like this to humans.

'Authority' has had a bad press, in much of the world, for 100 years and more now. It goes together, in the popular mind, with nasty ideas like 'repression', 'human rights abuses' and such like. Think of 'the authorities' and what do you see? Police officers, perhaps. Judges, looking stern and solemn, and ready to send you to prison. Faceless civil servants and bureaucrats, making laws and regulations which seem designed to make life difficult for ordinary people like you.

In some countries, 'the authorities' means something worse still. It means people who knock on your door at five o'clock in the morning, take you away with no good reason, beat you up and maybe kill you. It means people who pass oppressive laws that force you to leave your family for half the year if you want to find any work – or that prevent you from leaving your own town to find work in the next one, because a new border has just been drawn across the map of your own country. 'The authorities' are people who seem to be able to run things the way they want but are answerable to nobody.

What 'authority' really means in all these cases, of course, is 'people who have the power to do what they want'. This usually means 'people who have an army to back them up'. Authority means power, which means force, which means violence. No wonder we're suspicious of the very word 'authority' itself.

Yet here it is again in the gospel story: Jesus has authority. You can't miss it. Authority in his teaching. Authority over diseases at a distance. Authority over the storm, over the demons. Now, authority to do what normally only God does: to put away sins, to change a person's life from the inside out, to free him from whatever was gripping him so tightly that he couldn't move. What is this authority? Is it anything like the authorities we know in our world?

70

Supposing there was a different kind of authority. Supposing there was a different kind of power. A power that didn't work by having an army at its back and thugs to break down your door at five in the morning: a force that had nothing to do with violence, and everything to do with the strange compelling power of freedom and love. Let's have some of that, you say. Well, that's what's on offer in the gospel.

That's why Jesus' actions were so astonishingly effective – so much so that the people with a little bit of power of their own in his world were angry and upset. That's why Matthew is taking two whole chapters right now to tell us, in one story after another, that this is precisely the sort of authority that Jesus has (see verses 6 and 8). And that's why we need to pay special attention at this point. This is the sort of authority we could all do with.

At the heart of this story is Jesus' claim to forgive sins, to 'put them away' as the Jews often said. The word 'forgive' here literally means 'send away', sending all one's sins off into the far beyond where they are forgotten for ever. That, it seems, is what was needed in this case. In most of Jesus' healings this wasn't the issue, but it certainly was here.

A glance at the paralysed man on his stretcher told Jesus all he needed to know. This paralysis was the sort where what we would call psychological forces had reduced the body to immovability. The man had done something – perhaps many things – of which he was deeply ashamed. He was in over his head, as we say, and saw no way out. He not only felt guilty; he *was* guilty, and he knew it. And gradually this gnawing sense of guilt stopped him doing things. Then it stopped him moving his body altogether.

And finally his friends took their faith and their friend in their own hands and brought him to Jesus.

Once again, 'faith' here means 'faith in Jesus' authority'; 'faith that Jesus will be able to do something about it'. That's what Jesus is responding to. He addresses the key problem, knowing that all the symptoms will quickly disappear if the main disease is dealt with. Jesus has no straightforwardly physical means of healing the man. He uses the authority which God has invested in him, authority to forgive sins and so to bring new life. He is already acting as 'the son of man', the one who is to be enthroned over all the forces of evil (Daniel 7.13–14). He has the right, even in the present, to declare that sin is a beaten foe and to send it away.

Already in the story we can see, looming up ahead and inviting us forward to the climax of the book, the shape of Jesus' whole ministry. He has come as the son of man, the Messiah, Israel's representative. And he has come, not just to deal with the oppression caused by Rome, but to address the deeper and darker oppression caused by evil itself. Beyond that again, he has come to challenge evil's ultimate result, which is not just paralysis but death itself.

That's why, in this story, the language used three times over for what Jesus tells the paralysed man to do would remind Matthew's readers of language they were used to hearing in connection with Jesus' resurrection. 'Get up!' he says, and the man got up, 'arose'. When sin is dealt with, resurrection (at whatever level) can't be far behind.

We can also see, embedded in this story, some of the forces that put Jesus on the cross, and thus, unwittingly, contributed to his decisive victory over sin. Those who objected to his dramatic and authoritative announcement that the man's sins were put away were no doubt reckoning that this was something only God himself could do. God's normal way of doing it was through the Temple-system, through the established and authorized (that word again) priesthood. What they hadn't bargained for was that God would, when the great moment came, delegate this role to 'one like a son of man' through whom authority of the right sort would now be let loose in the world. But the forces of resistance, the forces that see their own power undermined by God's new sort of power, remain angry and obdurate. We shall see in this chapter how they begin to snipe at him and attack him, a process which will grow and swell until Jesus eventually stands before the high priest himself and makes, for the last time, a great statement about the authority of the son of man (26.64). After that, all that is left is his death, through which all sins were dealt with – and his own 'getting up', the sign, as in this story, that God was indeed with him, and had given him his own special type of authority, to heal and restore the world.

For Reflection or Discussion

What does this passage teach about authority? How and in what way is Jesus victorious over the forces of evil?

WEEK 3: WEDNESDAY

The Raising of the Little Girl: Matthew 9.18–26

[18]As Jesus was saying this, suddenly an official came up and knelt down in front of him.

'It's my daughter!' he said. 'She's just died! But – if you'll come and lay your hand on her, she'll come back to life!'

[19]Jesus got up and followed him. So did his disciples.

[20]Just then a woman appeared. She had suffered from internal bleeding for twelve years. She came up behind Jesus and touched the hem of his coat.

[21]'If I can only touch his coat,' she said to herself, 'I'll be rescued.'

[22]Jesus turned round and saw her.

'Cheer up, my daughter!' he said. 'Your faith has rescued you.' And the woman was healed from that moment.

[23]Jesus went into the official's house. There he saw the flute-players, and everybody in a great state of agitation.

[24]'Go away!' he said. 'The little girl isn't dead. She's asleep!' And they laughed at him.

[25]So when everybody had been put out, he went in and took hold of her hand, and she got up. [26]The report of this went out around the whole of that region.

As I write this, Britain's farms are in a state of crisis. A powerful disease has spread through tens of thousands of animals, which have had to be slaughtered. Much of the countryside is closed off; nobody is allowed to walk through fields and woods, or to exercise dogs near where livestock are kept. To gain access to a farming area you have to drive through piles of disinfected straw; if you are on foot, you have to walk through disinfectant. The disease brings horror everywhere it goes, and fear everywhere it might go. Suddenly everyone is taking very strict precautions about animal hygiene, though alas it seems too late.

All societies have hygiene regulations. Often we only notice them when, as in the farms just now, they have to be introduced all of a sudden. But we all learn when to wash our hands, and how to clean cups, plates and cutlery after using them. We don't usually give it a thought. If we did, we'd talk about germs, about infections, about staying healthy.

In societies before modern medicine, where you couldn't cure infections nearly as easily as we can now, it was vital to have strict codes about what you could and couldn't touch, and what to do if you did contract 'impurity'. These weren't silly regulations; they didn't mean you were being 'legalistic'. They were and are practical wisdom to keep society in good shape. The Jewish people, who had plenty of regulations like that in the Bible already, had codified them further to make it clearer to people exactly how to keep from getting sick. And two of the things that were near the top of the list, things to avoid if you wanted to stay 'pure' in that sense, were dead bodies on the one hand and women with internal bleeding (including menstrual periods) on the other. And in this double story Jesus is touched by a haemorrhaging woman, and then he himself touches a corpse.

No Jew would have missed the point – and Matthew was most likely writing for a largely Jewish audience. In the ordinary course of events, Jesus would have become doubly 'unclean', and would have had to bathe himself and his clothes and wait until the next day before resuming normal social contact. This was quite a usual process. Nobody would have given it much thought, any more than we comment on someone doing the laundry today. But when we read the story from this point of view what actually happened is all the more remarkable.

It all began with a flurry of activity, a man in a panic. He was an 'official' – probably a local civil servant or government agent. Normally such people would keep their dignity; they would walk with a measured tread and speak calmly to those they met. They had a social status to preserve. But this man has thrown all that out of the window. His little daughter has just died! What can he do? He's heard that there's a prophet in town who seems to be curing people – perhaps he can help! And before he quite knows what he's doing he's rushed out of his house, down the road to where Jesus stands with a crowd of people around him, and he's thrown himself down on the dusty road right there in front of all the neighbours. Who cares about dignity when your daughter's life is at stake?

The story keeps us in suspense while we switch attention from a little girl to an older woman. Having had her particular ailment – internal bleeding – for twelve years, she sees her chance of healing, and takes it. Knowing she is making everyone 'unclean' as she pushes past them, she comes up and touches Jesus.

But at this point we realize that something is different. Her 'uncleanness' doesn't infect him. Something in *him* infects *her*. Jesus turns round, sees her and tells her, as he told the centurion, that what has made the difference is her own faith (8.13; see 9.2, 29). Here is the mystery: Jesus has the power to heal, but those who receive it are those with faith. And the word Matthew uses for 'healing' in verses 21 and 22 is 'save', 'rescue'. No early Christian would miss the point. What Jesus was doing was the beginning of his whole work of rescuing the world, saving the world, from everything that polluted, defaced and destroyed it. And those who would benefit would be those who would believe.

The greatest destroyer is of course death itself. Here we see a stage further in Matthew's description of Jesus' healing work. The official's daughter is already dead, and the people in the house know it. They have already begun the sorrowful process of weeping and wailing, letting their grief have full vent over the lovely young life cut short. Jesus won't have it. Taking a huge risk – they are already laughing at him, and now he is going to go and touch the corpse – he holds the little girl's hand, and she gets up (again the word is a 'resurrection' word: she 'arose').

We in our modern world have many ways of dealing with personal impurity. Contemporary hygiene and chemicals mean we don't have to worry about it nearly as much as people in the ancient world. But, of course, some of the very chemicals we use, as we now know, pollute our atmosphere, our fields and our crops. Some of our contemporary pressure groups are just as worried about 'pollution' in this environmental sense as the Pharisees were with pollution as defined by their purity codes. The followers of Jesus may be called to find ways of dealing with such new pollutions, to explore new types of healing to bring cleansing and a new start to communities, agriculture and the very air we breathe.

But there are still other types of pollution as well: the pollution which gets into our minds and hearts, into our imagination and memory. How can we get rid of that? One way is to spend time with a story like this. Imagine yourself as an actor or actress in the drama. Suppose you were the official . . . or the woman with the internal bleeding . . . or one of the flute-players in the house . . . or one of the disciples, looking on . . .

Or, if you dare, suppose you were . . . Jesus himself . . .

For Reflection or Discussion

What is the context of Jesus' mission to cleanse us from pollution? How does it speak to you?

WEEK 3: THURSDAY

The Servant: Matthew 12.15–21

[15]Jesus discovered the plots against him, and left the district. Large crowds followed him, and he healed them all, [16]giving them strict instructions not to tell people about him. [17]This was so that what was spoken through Isaiah the prophet might come true:

> [18]Look! Here's my servant, whom I chose;
> my beloved one, my heart's delight.
> My spirit I will place on him,
> and he'll announce true judgment
> to the whole wide world.
> [19]He will not argue, nor will he
> lift up his voice and shout aloud;
> nobody in the streets will hear
> his voice. [20]He will not break the damaged
> reed, or snuff the guttering lamp,
> until his judgment wins the day.
> [21]The world will hope upon his name.

The bishop sat at his desk and put his head in his hands. Another three letters had just arrived complaining at the way in which a particular parish had changed its style of music. The director of finance had just reported that unless people in the diocese gave a lot more money in the next six months they would have to close some churches and make two or three priests redundant. The police were investigating a church worker following some serious allegations. One of the bishop's closest colleagues had just had a major operation and was beginning two months' sick leave. And now a telephone call had informed him that one of his own children was in trouble at school and he must come at once.

As he paused, his head spinning with all the bad news, there came into his mind the verse he'd heard at morning prayer an hour or so before. 'The world will hope upon his name.' Matthew, quoting Isaiah.

From somewhere – it seemed a long way away – he could see in his mind's eye an African village, where a young catechist was explaining to an eager group what it meant to follow Jesus' costly kingdom-way rather than to jump on the bandwagon of popular revolutionary movements. He saw, behind them, the hospital they had already built, the wells they had dug. Then he saw a huge congregation in Latin America, celebrating God's love in the middle of poverty and despair. He saw the dwindling churches of the Middle East, surrounded by hostile governments and religious pressure groups, facing problems nobody in the Western world could even imagine. He saw the faces of a young Pakistani couple he'd visited a few months previously, bringing their first child for baptism in a village church some miles outside Karachi. And, finally, he saw the teenagers he had confirmed the previous evening in a parish in his own diocese. These stories, he thought, are all telling The Story. The Story of one man, one name, one hope, one world. Somehow the letters and the telephone calls and the worrying reports are part of that Story as well. Somehow they belong.

And he felt, perhaps, something of what Matthew was trying to tell us in this passage. Here is Jesus, surrounded by pressures on all sides. His own followers don't yet really understand what he's doing. People are badgering him from every direction to heal them, to cast out evil spirits, to be there for them in their every need. At the same time, opposition is growing. Herod is not far away. Religious pressure groups are stirring up trouble. Some are even saying he's in league with the devil. He knows where it's all leading. And still he goes on.

And he goes on because he has a story in mind. The story of the Servant: Isaiah's story, the most famous story of the most famous prophet. The story of the Servant begins in the passage Matthew quotes here; it's taken from Isaiah 42. The 'Servant of YHWH' is a strange figure in Isaiah: one who will bring YHWH's blessing and justice to the world – the task which, earlier in Isaiah, was assigned to the Messiah, the coming king. But how is the Servant to accomplish his task? Not, it seems, by bullying and harrying Israel and the nations, by threatening and fighting. Rather, with a quiet and gentle work of healing, bearing the love and grace of God to the dark parts of Israel and the world.

Matthew looks back over the ministry of Jesus, knowing where it will lead. He sees Jesus as the Servant, not only when he dies a cruel death, wounded for our transgressions and bruised for our iniquities, but also in the *style* of what he is already doing in Galilee. He is going about bringing God's restoration wherever it is needed, not by making a fuss, but by gently leading people into God's healing love.

This is the story of one 'in whose name the nations will hope'. Well, they would, wouldn't they?

The nations – and, alas, Israel as well, as becomes clear in Matthew's story – are bent on violence and arrogance. Those who want peace and who work for it are always, in the end, shouted down by those who want more money, more land, more security, more status, and are prepared to fight and kill to get it. Those who are great and mighty in this world's terms make sure their voices are heard in the streets. Those who shout loudest get obeyed the soonest. But that's not the Servant's way.

So, too, those who want to get ahead in this world tend to push others out of the way. If they see a weak link – a rod that's bent and could break, a candle that's almost gone out – they will trample on it without a thought. That's not the Servant's way. The nations are used to arrogance. Here is a Servant who is the very opposite. He is the one shining light, the one hopeful sign.

And if the nations can hope in him, then hard-worked and hard-pressed church workers today – and all who come to the Bible, and who come to Jesus, looking for help – can find fresh hope in him. The bishop raised his head from his hands and looked around the room. All the problems were still there, and he was going to have a hard day dealing with them. But he was part of the Story, the Story of the Servant. And the Servant would be with him in all of them, bringing his gentle healing touch wherever it was needed.

For Reflection or Discussion

What are the characteristics of the Servant in Isaiah? How does the story shed light on what Jesus came to do?

WEEK 3: FRIDAY

The Challenge of Forgiveness: Matthew 18.21–35

[21]Then Peter came to Jesus.

'Master,' he said, 'how many times must I forgive my brother when he sins against me? As many as seven times?'

[22]'I wouldn't say seven times,' replied Jesus. 'Why not – seventy times seven?'

[23]'So, you see,' he went on, 'the kingdom of heaven is like a royal personage who wanted to settle up accounts with his servants. [24]As he was beginning to sort it all out, one man was brought before him who owed ten thousand talents. [25]He had no means of paying it back, so the master ordered him to be sold, with his wife and children and everything he possessed, and payment to be made.

[26]'So the servant fell down and prostrated himself before the master.

'"Be patient with me," he said, "and I'll pay you everything!"

[27]'The master was very sorry for the servant, and let him off. He forgave him the loan.

[28]'But that servant went out and found one of his fellow-servants, who owed him a hundred dinars. He seized him and began to throttle him. "Pay me back what you owe me!" he said.

[29]'The colleague fell down and begged him, "Be patient with me, and I'll pay you!"

[30]'But he refused, and went and threw him into prison until he could pay the debt.

[31]'So when his fellow-servants saw what had happened, they were very upset. They went and informed their master about the whole affair. [32]Then his master summoned him.

'"You're a scoundrel of a servant!" he said to him. "I let you off the whole debt, because you begged me to. [33]Shouldn't you have taken pity on your colleague, like I took pity on you?"

> [34]"His master was angry, and handed him over to the tor-
> turers, until he had paid the whole debt. [35]And that's what
> my heavenly father will do to you, unless each of you forgives
> your brother or sister from your heart.'

Many years ago I was working in a student community.
I sometimes assisted in leading worship or preaching for
one particular group of students. They were theological
students, training for ministry, but they shared their accom-
modation with others from a wide range of subjects – and
with a wide range of ideals and standards. I had agreed,
some while before, to preach at a midweek service in
which the assigned reading, as I knew long in advance, was
the passage we're now looking at. What none of us knew
was that it was going to be frighteningly relevant.

That week there was a near-riot. Some of the other
students living in the residence had been behaving very
disruptively. They were making it almost impossible for
their colleagues to sleep at night, to study during the day
or to have any peace and quiet. Most of the students
didn't even like to invite friends round because the place
was so unpleasant. A difficult atmosphere developed as
some of the Christian students simply wanted to 'forgive'
the troublemakers, in other words not to deal with the
problem, while others wanted to make an angry protest, to
demand their rights to live in peace and to insist that the
disruptive students were dismissed or at least suspended.

So on that weekday lunchtime, at our regular service,
you could have heard a pin drop when we heard Matthew
18.21–35 – the passage now in front of you – as the main
reading. And my heart was thumping as I stood up to
preach about it.

It's a long time ago, and sadly I can't find the notes of what I said. But the lesson of the story is so massive and obvious that I don't really need to look it up. There are several ways of putting the point. Every time you accuse someone else, you accuse yourself. Every time you forgive someone else, though, you pass on a drop of water out of the bucketful that God has already given you. From God's point of view, the distance between being ordinarily sinful (what we all are) and extremely sinful (what the people we don't like seem to be) is like the distance between London and Paris seen from the point of view of the sun. And so on. We can all relate to that.

The key thing, as I have already said, is not that one should therefore swallow all resentment and 'forgive and forget' as though nothing has happened. The key thing is that one should never, ever give up making forgiveness and reconciliation one's goal. If confrontation has to happen, as it often does, it must always be with forgiveness in mind, never revenge. It must always be with the aim of healing the wounded relationship, not leaving it to fester.

But underneath that there is another lesson, more subtle perhaps but equally important. Why does Jesus solemnly say, in the last verse, that those who refuse to forgive will themselves be refused forgiveness? Isn't that, to put it bluntly, so harsh as to be out of keeping with the rest of the gospel? Can't God override our failings at exactly that point?

Apparently not. At least, I don't know about 'can't', but it seems that he won't. The New Testament speaks with one voice on this subject. Forgiveness isn't like a Christmas present that a kindly grandfather can go ahead and give to a sulky grandchild even if the grandchild hasn't bought a single gift for anyone else. It isn't like the meal that will be waiting for you back home even if you failed to buy a cheese sandwich and a cup of tea for a tramp on the street. It's a different sort of thing altogether.

Forgiveness is more like the air in your lungs. There's only room for you to inhale the next lungful when you've just breathed out the previous one. If you insist on withholding it, refusing to give someone else the kiss of life he or she may desperately need, you won't be able to take any more in yourself, and you will suffocate very quickly. Whatever the spiritual, moral and emotional equivalent of the lungs may be (we sometimes say 'the heart', but that of course is a metaphor as well), it's either open or closed. If it's open, able and willing to forgive others, it will also be open to receive God's love and forgiveness. But if it's locked up to the one, it will be locked up to the other.

Peter's question and Jesus' answer say it all (verses 21–22). If you're still counting how many times you've forgiven someone, you're not really forgiving them at all, but simply postponing revenge. 'Seventy times seven' is a typical bit of Jesus' teasing. What he means, of course, is 'Don't even think about counting; just do it.'

For Reflection or Discussion

How can you becoming more forgiving? Why is the phrase 'forgive and forget' misleading?

WEEK 3: SATURDAY

Jesus Mocked and Crucified: Matthew 27.27–38

[27]Then the soldiers of the governor took Jesus into the barracks, and gathered the whole regiment together. [28]They took off

his clothes and dressed him up in a scarlet military cloak. [29]They wove a crown out of thorns and stuck it on his head, and put a reed in his right hand. Then they knelt down in front of him.

'Greetings, King of the Jews!' they said, making fun of him.

[30]They spat on him. Then they took the reed and beat him about the head. [31]When they had finished mocking him, they took off the cloak, dressed him in his own clothes again, and led him off to crucify him.

[32]As they were going out they found a man from Cyrene, called Simon. They forced him to carry his cross.

[33]When they came to the place called Golgotha, which means Skull-Place, [34]they gave him a drink of wine mixed with bitter herbs. When he tasted it, he refused to drink it.

[35]So then they crucified him. They divided up his clothes by casting lots, [36]and they sat down and kept watch over him there. [37]And they placed the written charge above his head: 'This is Jesus, the King of the Jews.'

[38]Then they crucified two brigands alongside him, one on his right and one on his left.

Almost the whole world is now a tourist trap. Countries compete with each other to attract visitors, particularly from the richer parts of the world, and to give them a memorable vacation while drawing money into the local economy.

The novelist Julian Barnes exploits this nicely in his novel *England, England*. He imagines the Isle of Wight – a small island just off the southern coast of England – being turned into a miniature version of the whole country, with all the familiar landmarks rebuilt there, and all the familiar events staged there. The busy tourist wouldn't have to bother going even to London, let alone to other well-known sites around the country. Everything would be there.

In the middle of it, Barnes imagines that a role would be found for the monarchy – which is, after all, what many tourists travel to England to see. There would be a king and queen, paid to live in a replica of one of the royal palaces. They would come out on to a balcony at regular times and wave to the crowds. 'Royal' events would be staged so that the tourists would feel they had seen something like the real thing. But of course it would all be a sham. Everybody would know that it was just a huge theme park.

The motive for doing it all, of course, would be money. The motive for the faked 'royal' events in this section of Matthew is more complex.

The soldiers mocking Jesus had nothing to gain financially by dressing him up as a king and pretending to salute him and kneel down before him. They had other things in mind. They had been fighting what today we would call terrorists – Jewish rebels against Rome, desperate for liberty, ready to do anything. The Roman soldiers had probably seen some of their friends killed. They were tired of policing such a place, far away from their homes, having to keep the lid on a volatile and dangerous situation with all kinds of rebel groups ready to riot.

Now here was someone who'd been accused of trying to make himself 'King of the Jews'. He was going to die within hours. Why not have a bit of fun at his expense? Why not tease him, beat him up a bit, show him what the Romans think of other people's 'kings'? Like the 'king' in

Julian Barnes's scaled-down England, let's let him know that someone else is in fact boss.

It's hard, reading this story, to remember that this is the same Jesus who, days before, was confronting the authorities in the Temple, and who, weeks before, was healing people, celebrating with people and teaching them about God's kingdom. But Matthew has woven hints of all that into the story, to remind us of how Jesus' crucifixion was not a messy accident at the end of a glittering career, but was in fact the proper, though shocking, climax to it.

It isn't just that Jesus is 'enthroned', as it were, on the cross, with the title Matthew wants us to see as the true one written above his head. That, to be sure, is striking in itself. Condemned prisoners regularly had a placard above them, indicating their crime. What for Pilate and the soldiers was Jesus' 'crime' – his claim to be Israel's true king – was for Matthew the sober truth. And the crucifixion was the means by which his kingdom would be established. As he had said to James and John (20.23), there would come a time when he would indeed be enthroned with one person on his right and another on his left; but the throne he had in mind was the cross.

Why? Because the kingdom Jesus had spoken of, from the Sermon on the Mount onwards, was never a kingdom to be established and maintained by military force. If it was to be God's kingdom, it would come about by God's means; and the means that the true God chooses to use are the means of self-giving love. Notice how, in this passage, parts of the Sermon on the Mount come back into play. Jesus himself, at last, is struck about the face by the soldiers and doesn't retaliate (Matthew 5.39). They take off his outer and inner garments, leaving him naked (Matthew 5.40). As he is going out to be crucified, the soldiers use their 'right' under Roman law to compel someone to carry a burden for them, just as in Matthew 5.41; only this time the burden in question is the heavy cross-beam on which Jesus will be hung.

The point of it all is this: Jesus is leading the way he had spoken of from the beginning, the way of being God's true Israel, the light of the world. He himself is set on a hill, unable now to remain hidden (5.14). This is how he is shining the light of God's love into the dark corners of the world: by taking the evil of the world, the hatred and cruelty and unthinking mockery of the world, the gratuitous violence, bullying and torture that still defaces the world, and letting it do its worst to him. Never let it be said that the Christian faith is an airy-fairy thing, all about having wonderful inner, spiritual experiences, and not about the real world. This story takes us to the very heart of what Christianity is all about; and here we meet, close up and raw, the anger and bitterness of the world, doing its worst against one who embodies and represents the love of the creator God himself.

And now, how do we respond as we stand and watch this shocking, tragic and yet deeply healing event?

We are of course outraged that such things should happen. Yes, Jesus will say to us, and they are still happening around the world today; what are we doing about it?

We are also horrified that such things should happen to Jesus himself, this Jesus who had done so many wonderful things, through whom healing and restoration, forgiveness and love came so freely to so many. Yes, Jesus will say to us, and this enthronement now will bring healing, forgiveness and hope to millions more. Do we know it ourselves, and if so are we helping others to know it too?

For Reflection or Discussion

How do you respond to the cross? How does it touch your life?

WEEK 4: A TIME TO LOVE

FOURTH SUNDAY OF ADVENT

The Birth of Jesus: Matthew 1.18–25

[18]This was how the birth of Jesus the Messiah took place. His mother, Mary, was engaged to Joseph; but before they came together she turned out to be pregnant – by the holy spirit. [19]Joseph, her husband-to-be, was an upright man. He didn't want to make a public example of her. So he decided to set the marriage aside privately. [20]But, while he was considering this, an angel of the Lord suddenly appeared to him in a dream.

'Joseph, son of David,' the angel said, 'Don't be afraid to get married to Mary. The child she is carrying is from the holy spirit. [21]She is going to have a son. You must give him the name Jesus; he is the one who will save his people from their sins.'

[22]All this happened so that what the Lord said through the prophet might be fulfilled: [23]'Look: the virgin is pregnant, and will have a son, and they shall give him the name Emmanuel,' – which means, in translation, 'God with us.'

[24]When Joseph woke up from his sleep he did what the Lord's angel had told him to. He married his wife, [25]but he didn't have sexual relations with her until after the birth of her son. And he gave him the name Jesus.

One of the most memorable movies I have seen is the film of Charles Dickens's novel *Little Dorrit*. It is actually two films, both very long. The two films don't follow in sequence, telling the first and second halves of the story; instead, each film shows the whole drama, but from a different point of view. First we see the action through the eyes of the hero; then, in the second film, the same story through the eyes of the heroine. A few scenes are identical, but in the second film we understand many things that hadn't been clear first time around. Like seeing with two eyes instead of one, the double movie enables the viewer to get a sense of depth and perspective on the whole dramatic story.

The story of Jesus' birth in Matthew's gospel is seen through the eyes of Joseph; in Luke's gospel, we see it through Mary's. No attempt is made to bring them into line. The central fact is the same; but instead of Luke's picture of an excited Galilean girl, learning that she is to give birth to God's Messiah, Matthew shows us the more sober Joseph, discovering that his fiancée is pregnant. The only point where the two stories come close is when the angel says to Joseph, as Gabriel said to Mary, 'Don't be afraid.' That is an important word for us, too, as we read the accounts of Jesus' birth.

Fear at this point is normal. For centuries now many opponents of Christianity, and many devout Christians themselves, have felt that these stories are embarrassing and unnecessary – and untrue. We know (many will say) that miracles don't happen. Remarkable healings, perhaps; there are ways of explaining them. But not babies born without human fathers. This is straining things too far.

Some go further. These stories, they say, have had an unfortunate effect. They have given the impression that sex is dirty and that God doesn't want anything to do with it. They have given rise to the legend that Mary stayed a virgin for ever (something the Bible never says; indeed, here and elsewhere it implies that she and Joseph lived a normal married life after Jesus' birth). This has promoted the belief that virginity is better than marriage. And so on.

It is of course true that strange ideas have grown up around the story of Jesus' conception and birth, but Matthew (and Luke) can hardly be blamed for that. They were telling the story they believed was both true and the ultimate explanation of why Jesus was the person he was.

They must have known that they were taking a risk. In the ancient pagan world there were plenty of stories of heroes conceived by the intervention of a god, without a human father. Surely Matthew, with his very Jewish perspective on everything, would hardly invent such a thing, or copy it from someone else unless he really believed it. Wouldn't it be opening Christianity to the sneers of its opponents, who would quickly suggest the obvious alternative, namely that Mary had become pregnant through some more obvious but less reputable means?

Well, yes, it would; but that would only be relevant if nobody already knew that there had been something strange about Jesus' conception. In John's gospel we hear the echo of a taunt made during Jesus' lifetime: maybe, the crowds suggest, Jesus' mother had been misbehaving before her marriage (8.41). It looks as though Matthew and Luke are telling this story because they know rumours have circulated and they want to set the record straight.

Alternatively, people have suggested that Matthew made his story up so that it would present a 'fulfilment' of the passage he quotes in verse 23, from Isaiah 7.14. But, interestingly, there is no evidence that anyone before Matthew saw that verse as something that would have to be fulfilled by the coming Messiah. It looks rather as though he found the verse because he already knew the story, not the other way round.

Everything depends, of course, on whether you believe that the living God could, or would, act like that. Some say he couldn't ('Miracles don't happen'); others that he wouldn't ('If he did that, why doesn't he intervene to stop genocide?'). Some say Joseph, and others at the time, didn't know the scientific laws of nature the way we do – though this story gives the lie to that, since if Joseph hadn't known how babies were normally made he wouldn't have had a problem with Mary's unexpected pregnancy.

But Matthew and Luke don't ask us to take the story all by itself. They ask us to see it in the light both of the entire history of Israel – in which God's love was always present and at work, often in very surprising ways – and, more particularly, of the subsequent story of Jesus himself. Does the rest of the story, and the impact of Jesus on the world and countless individuals within it ever since, make it more or less likely that he was indeed conceived by a special act of the holy spirit?

That is a question everyone must answer for themselves. But Matthew wouldn't want us to stop there. He wants to tell us more about who Jesus was and is, in a time-honoured Jewish fashion: by his special names. The name Jesus was a popular boy's name at the time, being in Hebrew the same as Joshua, who brought the Israelites into the promised land after the death of Moses. Matthew sees Jesus as the one who will now complete what the law of Moses pointed to but could not of itself produce. He will rescue his people, not from slavery in Egypt, but from

94

the slavery of sin, the 'exile' they have suffered not just in Babylon but in their own hearts and lives.

By contrast, the name Emmanuel, mentioned in Isaiah 7.14 and 8.8, was not given to anyone else, perhaps because it would say more about a child than anyone would normally dare. It means 'God with us'. Matthew's whole gospel is framed by this theme: at the very end, Jesus promises that he will be 'with' his people to the close of the age (28.20). The two names together express the meaning of the story. God is present, with his people; he doesn't 'intervene' from a distance, but is always active, expressing his love in unexpected ways. And God's actions are aimed at rescuing people from a helpless plight, demanding that he take the initiative and do things people had regarded as (so to speak) inconceivable.

This is the God, and this is the Jesus, whose boundless love for the world is expressed in the story that Matthew sets before us.

For Reflection or Discussion

What do you believe about Jesus' conception and why? How does this passage help you?

WEEK 4: MONDAY

Loving Your Enemies: Matthew 5.38–48

[38]"You heard that it was said, "An eye for an eye, and a tooth for a tooth." [39]But I say to you: don't use violence to resist evil! Instead, when someone hits you on the right cheek, turn the other one towards him. [40]When someone wants to sue you and take your shirt, let him have your cloak, too. [41]And when someone forces you to go one mile, go a second one

with him. [42]Give to anyone who asks you, and don't refuse someone who wants to borrow from you.

[43]"You heard that it was said, "Love your neighbour and hate your enemy." [44]But I tell you: love your enemies! Pray for people who persecute you! [45]That way, you'll be children of your father in heaven! After all, he makes his sun rise on bad and good alike, and sends rain both on the upright and on the unjust. [46]Look at it like this: if you love those who love you, do you expect a special reward? Even tax-collectors do that, don't they? [47]And if you only greet your own family, what's so special about that? Even Gentiles do that, don't they? [48]Well then: you must be perfect, just as your heavenly father is perfect.'

There was once a father who had to go away from his young family for three or four days on business. Anxious that his wife should be properly looked after in his absence, he had a word with the oldest son, who was nine at the time.

'When I'm away,' he said, 'I want you to think what I would normally do around the house, and you do it for me.' He had in mind, of course, clearing up in the kitchen, washing up dishes, putting out the rubbish, and similar tasks.

On his return, he asked his wife what the son had done. 'Well,' she said, 'it was very strange. Straight after breakfast he made himself another cup of coffee, went into the living room, put on some loud music, and read the newspaper for half an hour.' The father was left wondering whether his son had obeyed him a bit too accurately.

The shocking thing about this passage in the Sermon on the Mount is that we are told to watch what our heavenly father is doing and then do the same ourselves. Here is the puzzle: Israel, the chosen people, are challenged to realize that God doesn't have favourites! What sense can we make of that? If they are chosen, doesn't that mean they are God's favourites?

The answer to the puzzle is found earlier in the Sermon. Israel isn't chosen in order to be God's special people while the rest of the world remains in outer darkness. Israel is chosen to be the light of the world, the salt of the earth. Israel is chosen so that, through Israel, God can bless all people. And now Jesus is calling Israel to *be* the light of the world at last. He is opening the way, carving a path through the jungle towards that vocation, urging his followers to come with him on the dangerous road.

And dangerous it is. Not only has Israel in Jesus' day got many enemies, pagan nations who have overrun the land and made the people subject to harsh rules and taxes. There are just as many dangers within, as movements of national resistance spring up, fuelled by anger at the increasing injustice and wickedness. And, within that again, the divisions within Jewish society are becoming more marked, with a few becoming very rich and the majority being poor, some very poor.

These were all pressing issues for the people listening to Jesus. How did his kingdom-message apply to them? How can it then apply to us today?

Jesus offers *a new sort of justice*, a creative, healing, restorative justice. The old justice found in the Bible was designed to prevent revenge running away with itself. Better an eye for an eye and a tooth for a tooth than an escalating feud with each side going one worse than the other. But Jesus goes one better still. Better to have no vengeance at all, but rather a creative way forward, reflecting the astonishingly patient love of God himself, who wants Israel to shine his light into the world so that all people will see that he is the one true God, and that his deepest nature is overflowing love. No other god encourages people to behave in a way like this!

So Jesus gives three hints of the sort of thing he has in mind. To be struck on the right cheek, in that world, almost certainly meant being hit with the back of the right hand. That's not just violence, but an insult: it implies that you're an inferior, perhaps a slave, a child or (in that world, and sometimes even today) a woman. What's the answer? Hitting back only keeps the evil in circulation. Offering the other cheek implies: hit me again if you like, but now as an equal, not an inferior.

Or suppose you're in a law court where a powerful enemy is suing you (perhaps for non-payment of some huge debt) and wants the shirt off your back. You can't win; but you can show him what he's really doing. Give him your cloak as well; and, in a world where most people only wore those two garments, shame him with your impoverished nakedness. This is what the rich, powerful and careless are doing. They are reducing the poor to a state of shame.

The third example clearly reflects the Roman military occupation. Roman soldiers had the right to force civilians to carry their equipment for one mile. But the law was quite strict; it forbade them to make someone go more than that. Turn the tables on them, advises Jesus. Don't fret and fume and plot revenge. Copy your generous God! Go a second mile, and astonish the soldier (and perhaps alarm him – what if his commanding officer found out?) with the news that there is a different way to be human, a way which doesn't plot revenge, which doesn't join the armed resistance movement (that's what verse 39 means), but which wins God's kind of victory over violence and injustice.

These examples are only little sketches, like cartoons to give you the idea. Whatever situation you're in, you need to think it through for yourself. What would it mean to reflect God's generous love despite the pressure and provocation, despite your own anger and frustration?

Impossible? Well, yes, at one level. But again Jesus' teaching isn't just good advice, it's good *news*. Jesus did it all himself, and opened up the new way of being human so that all who follow him can discover it. When they mocked him, he didn't respond. When they challenged him, he told quizzical, sometimes humorous, stories that forced them to think differently. When they struck him, he took the pain. When they put the worst bit of Roman equipment on his back – the heavy cross-piece on which he would be killed – he carried it out of the city to the place of his own execution. When they nailed him to the cross, he prayed for them.

The Sermon on the Mount isn't just about us. If it was, we might admire it as a fine bit of idealism, but we'd then return to our normal lives. It's about Jesus himself. This was the blueprint for his own life. He asks nothing of his followers that he hasn't faced himself. And, within his own life, we can already sense a theme that will grow larger and larger until we can't miss it. If this is the way to show what God is really like, and if this is the pattern that Jesus himself followed exactly, Matthew is inviting us to draw the conclusion: that in Jesus we see the Emmanuel, the God-with-us person. The Sermon on the Mount isn't just about how to behave. It's about discovering the living God in the loving, and dying, Jesus, and learning to reflect that love ourselves into the world that needs it so badly.

For Reflection or Discussion

What is the nature of the justice Jesus offers? How does his teaching on reflecting the generous God and defusing violence speak to you?

WEEK 4: TUESDAY

On Fasting and Lasting Treasure: Matthew 6.16–24

[16]'When you fast, don't be gloomy like the play-actors. They make their faces quite unrecognizable, so that everyone can see they're fasting. I'm telling you the truth: they have received their reward in full. [17]No: when you fast, tidy your hair and beard the way you normally do, and wash your face, [18]so that others won't notice you're fasting – except your father, privately. Then your father, who sees in private, will repay you.

[19]'Don't store up treasure on earth. Moths and rust will eat it away, and robbers will break in and steal it. [20]No: store up for yourselves treasure in heaven! Moths and rust don't eat it away there, and no robbers break in and steal it. [21]Show me your treasure, and I'll show you where your heart is.

[22]'The eye is the lamp of the body. So if your eye is honest and clear, your whole body will be full of light. [23]But if your eye is evil, your whole body is in the dark. So, if the light within you turns out to be darkness, darkness doesn't come any darker than that.

[24]'Nobody can serve two masters. Otherwise, they will either hate the first and love the second, or be devoted to the first and despise the second. You can't serve both God and wealth.'

The student looked crestfallen, as well he might. For weeks he had thought he was doing all right. Yes, he hadn't been working as hard as he could have done; but he was in the college football team, and he was playing in a rock group, and he was reading some very exciting novels . . . and somehow he hadn't been spending quite as much time in the library as most of the others. Now his tutor was facing him with the question. What were his priorities? Did he want to get a university education and degree, or did he just want to be at a wonderful holiday camp?

Of course, many students manage to juggle dozens of different commitments and still end up doing enough work to earn a degree. But frequently they have to face difficult choices. A bright, energetic young person could in theory do any one of several dozen things in any given week, but there are only so many hours in the day and you can't do everything. What is really important? What will you say, when you look back in ten years' time? 'I wish I'd really given it my best shot'? or 'I'm glad I decided to put all my effort into it'?

This passage is about priorities, and the central priority is God himself. No question about the importance of putting God first. But the catch is that, because God is loving and gentle, and wants us to choose to love and serve him freely rather than to be forced into it like slaves, it often seems, even to Christians who have in principle decided to give their lives to him, that there are many different things they could do. And often the different things start to take over . . . not least when they make money or bring fame. This passage is all about learning to love and serve God for himself, and in secret, rather than simply having an eye on the main chance, either to show off by being so religious or to store up wealth.

The opening paragraph picks up the same theme that we found in the earlier passages about money and prayer. Jesus assumes that his followers are going to fast from time to time, as part of their prayer and devotion to God. Later on (9.14–15) he explains that this won't be the right thing to do while he is there with them, but hints that it will be once he's gone. But the question is, how?

The current practice of Jesus' day seems to have been to advertise your fasting by letting your hair (and beard) go tangled, and by smearing ashes on your face. That's just play-acting, Jesus declares. It's putting on a mask. Real fasting is between you and God, not something you do to show off. So do what you normally do to your head and face – wash, comb, sort yourself out in the usual way (in his culture that included anointing with oil, and that's what this passage literally means). The important point, here and all through, is the question: is your eye fixed on God or on someone (or something) else? What is your priority?

The three little sayings which follow all make the same point. First, Jesus points out the difference between two sorts of treasure. As with other references to heaven and earth, we shouldn't imagine he means 'don't worry about this life – get ready for the next one'. 'Heaven' here is where God is right now, and where, if you learn to love and serve God right now, you will have treasure in the present, not just in the future. Of course, Jesus (like almost all Jews of his day) believed that after death God would have a wonderful future in store for his faithful people; but they didn't normally refer to that future as 'heaven'. He wanted his followers to establish heavenly treasure right now, treasure which they could enjoy in the present as well as the future, treasure that wasn't subject to the problems that face all earthly hoards. How can one do this? Well, the whole chapter so far gives us the clue. Learn to live in the presence of the loving father. Learn to do everything for him and him alone. Get your priorities right.

Second, make sure your lamp is shedding light, not darkness. This is a tricky little saying. What does Jesus mean by saying that the eye is the lamp of the body?

Three things, I think. First, he means that we must, as we say, 'keep our eyes fixed on God'. Since we can't actually see God, that is picture-language, but we know what he means.

Second, though, I think Jesus literally meant that we should take care what we actually look at. Where do your eyes naturally get drawn to? Are you in control of them, or do they take you – and your mind and heart – wherever they want?

Third, the eyes are like the headlights of a car. Supposing you're driving along a dark road at night and you try to switch the lights on – and nothing happens! You suddenly realize just how dark it really is. That's what it's like, Jesus is saying, if your eyes are not on God, and if instead they are following whatever eye-catching, pretty thing happens to take their fancy. Priorities again. Are your eyes leading you in the right direction and showing you the road ahead?

Finally, the best known of these sayings. You can't serve God and . . . mammon, say the older translations. 'Mammon' was a way of referring to property and wealth in general, almost as though it were a god – which is precisely Jesus' point here. We make the same point by saying things like 'the Almighty Dollar' (dangerously like 'Almighty God'). We joke about money because we are all too aware of its power: 'Money talks,' says the comedian, 'but what it mostly says to me is, "Goodbye!"' But what Jesus is saying is that money gives orders. It bosses you around. If you have your priorities right, there is only one boss, and that is God himself.

Sort your priorities out. Work out what you truly value, what you truly love.

For Reflection or Discussion

What are your real priorities? When you look back at your life in two, five, ten, fifteen years' time, will you be glad you put first things first?

WEEK 4: WEDNESDAY

Jesus Causes Division: Matthew 10.32–42

[32]'So: everyone who owns up in front of others to being on my side, I will own them before my father in heaven. [33]But anyone who disowns me in front of others, I will disown that person before my father in heaven.

[34]'Don't think it's my job to bring peace on the earth. I didn't come to bring peace – I came to bring a sword! [35]I came to divide a man from his father, a daughter from her mother, and a daughter-in-law from her mother-in-law. [36]Yes, you'll find your enemies inside your own front door.

[37]'If you love your father or mother more than me, you don't deserve me. If you love your son or daughter more than me, you don't deserve me. [38]Anyone who doesn't pick up their cross and follow after me doesn't deserve me. [39]If

you find your life you'll lose it, and if you lose your life because of me you'll find it.

[40]'Anyone who welcomes you, welcomes me; and anyone who welcomes me, welcomes the one who sent me. [41]Anyone who welcomes a prophet in the name of a prophet will receive a prophet's reward; and anyone who receives an upright person in the name of an upright person will receive an upright person's reward. [42]Anyone who gives even a cup of cold water to one of these little ones, in the name of a disciple – I'm telling you the truth, they won't go short of their reward!'

I was once asked to go and preach at the school which I had attended as a boy. It was one of those annual events that many schools have where we were supposed to remember the great pioneers who had founded the school, developed it and given it its character.

So that's what I preached about. But I pointed out that something very odd was going on. Each one of the men and women we were honouring had been innovators. They had been the ones who dared to do things differently, to go in a new direction despite the people who wanted to keep things as they were. But we, by reading out a list of their names in a solemn voice, and by holding them up as our founding figures, were in danger of doing the opposite: of saying that we wanted everything to stay just the way it had always been. Do you honour the memory of an innovator by slavishly following what he or she did, or by daring to be different in your turn?

The sermon caused, I think, a mild stir. But it was nothing like the stir which Jesus meant these words to cause. 'Sons against fathers, daughters against mothers' – what on earth could he mean? Rejecting parents and children – not peace on earth, but a sword – can this be

Jesus himself? What's going on? How can we get our minds around these strange sayings?

Of course, the New Testament also has a good deal to say about caring for one another within the family. And I know that some have misguidedly taken passages like these as a licence to neglect their own dependants and spend all their time on 'the Lord's work'. But these are stern and uncomfortable words which we can't ignore. They echo down the years into the Christian church of today.

Think of St Francis, leaving his wealthy home despite his father's fury, to go and live a simple life of imitating Jesus as much as he could – and setting an example that thousands still follow today.

Think of those who have faced terrible dangers for the sake of the gospel and have had to send their families to a place of safety elsewhere, while they have stayed to look after a church because there wasn't anyone else to do it.

Jesus doesn't say here that everyone who follows him will find themselves split off from their families; certainly not. Indeed, many of the apostles, in the days of the early church, took their spouses with them on their travels (1 Corinthians 9.5). But Jesus is once again talking about priorities, and is making remarkable and quite drastic claims.

He isn't saying (as some have tried to pretend that he was saying) that what matters is following God in your own way. He is saying, loud and clear, that what matters is allegiance to him: allegiance to Jesus must come at the top of every priority list. We can see, as the story unwinds, how difficult this was even for those who knew him personally: Peter denied him, Judas betrayed him, the rest all ran away and hid. But the challenge remains, embracing everything, demanding everything, offering everything, promising everything.

The absolute demand of Jesus brings us back to where we were in the Sermon on the Mount. It isn't the case that there are some fine ideals in the mind of God, and that Jesus just happens to teach them a bit better than most people. Nor is it the case that Jesus came to show the way through the present world to a quite different one, where we will go after death. No: Jesus came to begin and establish *the new way of being God's people*, and not surprisingly those who were quite happy with the old one, thank you very much, didn't like having it disturbed. He didn't want to bring division within households for the sake of it. But he knew that, if people followed his way, division was bound to follow.

Actually, the passage about sons and fathers, daughters and mothers, and so on, is a quotation from one of the Old Testament prophets (Micah 7.6). In this passage, the prophet predicts the terrible divisions that would always occur when God was doing a new thing. When God acts to rescue his people, there are always some who declare that they don't need rescuing, that they are comfortable as they are. Part of the reason for quoting this passage here is to say: don't be surprised if this happens now; this, too, is part of your tradition! Your own scriptures contain warnings about the great disruptions that will happen when God finally acts once and for all to save you.

That's why Jesus' challenge, to the disciples themselves and, through them, to the Israel of his day, had to be so sharp – and often has to be just as sharp today, where people still naturally prefer comfort to challenge. But the challenge of Jesus' sayings is matched by the remarkable promises he makes to those who accept them and live by them. He will 'own' us before his father in heaven. Those who lose their lives will find them. And, at the end, we have the remarkable chain reaction of those who serve their fellow human beings out of love for Jesus. Give a cup of cold water to one of Jesus' least significant followers, and you're giving it to Jesus himself; whatever you do for Jesus, you do, not just for Jesus, but for God ('the one who sent me'). If Jesus' people today could relearn this simple but profound lesson, the church might once again be able to go out with a message to challenge and change people's hearts.

For Reflection or Discussion

How can you put Jesus first in your life? What practical changes do you need to make?

WEEK 4: THURSDAY

The Great Commandment: Matthew 22.34–40

[34]When the Pharisees heard that Jesus had silenced the Sadducees, they got together in a group. [35]One of them, a lawyer, put him on the spot with this question.

[36]'Teacher,' he said, 'which is the most important commandment in the law?'

[37]'You must love the Lord your God', replied Jesus, 'with all your heart, with all your life, and with all your mind. [38]This is the first commandment, and it's the one that really matters. [39]The second is similar, and it's this: You must love your neighbour as yourself. [40]The entire law hangs on these two commandments – and that goes for the prophets, too.'

I watched on television a tennis match between two of the game's finest players. Both had been playing well, but towards the end one of them seemed to rise to new heights. The match ended with two stunning games, when the winner not only did everything right but superlatively. First his opponent served, and each serve was met with a return that won the point. Then, when it was his turn to serve, each one was a clean ace. Game, set and match.

That's how the end of Matthew 22 is meant to strike us. The answer the opponents couldn't question was followed by the question they couldn't answer. Which is the greatest commandment, they asked. Jesus' answer was so traditional that nobody could challenge him on it, and so deeply searching that everyone else would be challenged by it. Then it was Jesus' turn: is the Messiah David's son or David's master – or perhaps both? They'd never asked that question before, and they certainly didn't know the answer, even though it was standing in front of them in flesh and blood.

The next occasions when Jesus will meet his opponents will be in the garden when they arrest him, in the Council when they accuse him and on the cross when they mock him. But each time they will know, he will know, and we as Matthew's readers will know, that he knows the answers to these questions and they do not. He also knows, and Matthew wants us to know as well, that his arrest, trial and crucifixion are precisely the way in which Jesus is fulfilling the two great commandments, and the way in which he is being enthroned both as David's son, the true king of Israel, and David's master, David's Lord. This is how, as the son of God in a still fuller sense, he has come to rescue his people. Unless we are prepared to see these questions in this light we will remain shallow in our understanding of them.

Let's deal with the surface level, though, because that matters greatly as well. Many Jewish teachers posed the question as to which was the greatest out of all the 613 commandments in the law of Moses. Many would have agreed substantially with the answer that Jesus gave. Equally important, though, these commandments were not simply among the things the Jews were supposed to *do*. They formed part of the *prayer* that every devout Jew prayed every day, in a tradition that continues unbroken to the present time.

But did people actually keep these commandments? Jesus has already spoken, in chapter 15, of the need for the heart to be renewed so that people will produce words and deeds which are appropriate, rather than making them impure. His challenge in the Sermon on the Mount was that the heart should be renewed, not just that the outward actions should conform with the proper standard.

But how could this be done? Even those of us who have spent our whole lives trying to follow Jesus and live by his grace and love know that the heart doesn't seem to get renewed all in one go. Many, many bits of darkness and impurity still lurk in its depths, and sometimes take a lot of work, prayer and counsel to dig out and replace with the love which we all agree should really be there.

Once more, what Jesus says here about loving God, and loving one another, only makes sense when we set it within Matthew's larger gospel picture, of Jesus dying for the sins of the world and rising again with the message of new life. That's when these commandments begin to come into their own: when they are seen not as orders to be obeyed in our own strength, but as invitations and promises to a new way of life in which, bit by bit, hatred and pride can be left behind and love can become a reality.

For Reflection or Discussion

How does Jesus fulfil the two great commandments? Does it help you to see the commandments as invitations and promises?

WEEK 4: FRIDAY

Preparations for Jesus' Death: Matthew 26.1–13

¹So this is how it finally happened.

When Jesus had finished all these sayings, he said to his disciples, ²'In two days' time, as you know, it'll be Passover! That's when the son of man will be handed over to be crucified.'

³Then the chief priests got together with the elders of the people, in the official residence of the high priest, who was called Caiaphas. ⁴They plotted how to capture Jesus by some trick, and kill him.

⁵'We'd better not try anything at the feast,' they said. 'We don't want the people to riot.'

⁶While Jesus was at Bethany, in the house of Simon (known as 'the Leper'), ⁷a woman came to him who had an alabaster vase of extremely valuable ointment. She poured it on his head as he was reclining at the table.

⁸When the disciples saw it, they were furious.

'What's the point of all this waste?' they said. ⁹'This could have been sold for a fortune, and the money could have been given to the poor!'

¹⁰Jesus knew what they were thinking.

'Why make life difficult for the woman?' he said. 'It's a lovely thing, what she's done for me. [11]You always have the poor with you, don't you? But you won't always have me. [12]When she poured this ointment on my body, you see, she did it to prepare me for my burial. [13]I'm telling you the truth: wherever this gospel is announced in all the world, what she has just done will be told, and people will remember her.'

I stood at the bottom of the rock face. It was cold. The sun never penetrated that side of the mountain. I looked at the massive boulders around the foot of the climb, and then let my eye wander up the different routes, made famous by television programmes and glossy books as well as in specialist climbing literature. Up, and up, and up went the rock. I could just make out, as tiny coloured dots way above me, two or three groups of climbers. Some had started in the small hours that morning. One group had obviously begun the previous day. They had spent the night tied to the rock half a mile up, and were now making further progress.

I couldn't see the summit. There were clouds swirling around it. Though the forecast was good for later in the day, it was notorious that the weather could change suddenly, particularly up at the top.

Of all the mountains in Switzerland, the Eiger is the most stunning in its sheer, massive bulk. Its north face, at whose foot I was standing, looks as though some enormous giant had taken an axe and sliced through the mountain range, cutting away what might have been an ordinary, more gentle northern side, sloping down with meadows and woodland. Instead, what is left is this shocking vertical wall of bare rock, more than a mile high, blocking out the sun, simultaneously compelling and terrifying. I am drawn to it as by a magnet. Though my climbing days are long past, I can well understand why people want to spend days risking their lives to attempt it.

That is how we should feel as we stand at the foot of the final ascent of St Matthew's gospel. We have walked at a steady pace through the hills and valleys of the story. We have sat down to hear Jesus deliver another parable or discourse. We have marched with him along the road, enjoying the sunshine of the early days in Galilee and the remarkable views as the disciples gradually realized more of what the kingdom was about. We have arrived in Jerusalem and watched dramatic events unfold. But we are now standing in front of a sheer wall of rock, and if we don't find it both compelling and terrifying we haven't got the right spectacles on.

The death of Jesus of Nazareth is one of the most famous and formative events in human history. There is a lot to be said, before you begin to study it line by line, for first running your eye right up the wall of rock, for reading the next two chapters through at a single sitting, with the door shut and the telephone turned off. Allow the whole thing to make its proper impact on you.

The way Matthew has told it, the story is dizzying. Instead of the gentle mountain slope that might have been there – Jesus, after confronting the authorities, going off back to Galilee to talk of the birds of the sky and the lilies of the field, to teach people to pray, to become a venerable old prophet with a long grey beard – it is as though a giant has sliced through the story with an axe from top to bottom, leaving, like dark exposed rock, the raw emotions, the longings and the horrors, of dozens of individuals and, out beyond them, of Israel, of the world, of ourselves.

The top isn't always visible. It's often hidden in the clouds. I have spent most of my life trying to pray, think, speak and write about the meaning of the death of Jesus; and, to be honest, some days I think I can see it clearly and other days I can't. Mountains are like that, and so is theology. That doesn't mean you can't be sure that it's there and that it really matters. If you thought the summit of the Eiger was only 'there' when it wasn't shrouded in mist, you'd be making a bad mistake. The theories about why Jesus died – theories of the 'atonement', as they are called – are like maps or old photographs, taken from a distance. They may be accurate in their way, and they're helpful particularly when it's cloudy and you can't see too much for the moment. But they're not the same thing as climbing to the top yourself, and perhaps, if you're lucky, getting there on a clear day when you can see the view. When that happens, you will find you quickly run out of words to describe what you are looking at.

As with any mountain, there are always people who tried to climb it, who got halfway up, thought better of it and came back to declare that it was impossible and not worth doing anyway. Some people, including (alas) some within the church, would do anything rather than stand at the top of this mile-high rock, looking squarely at the death of Jesus in all its stark horror, and letting its beauty and terror captivate them for ever. But believe me, it's worth it. And Matthew is a great guide, if we will let him take us step by step.

The steps he shows us include a remarkable cast of characters, each of whom helps us a little way further towards the summit. Sometimes stories in the gospels are really only about Jesus and one or two others, but these two chapters are swarming with extra people. We hear their voices, see them plotting and squabbling and pontificating and weeping. We sense their excitement and panic, their politicking and puzzlement, their shock and trauma and hatred and hope.

Matthew allows each of them their say, and keeps them in balance: the central characters like Caiaphas and Peter, the walk-on parts like Pilate's wife and the servant-girls who point at Peter, the dark figure of Judas and the angry blaspheming pair crucified alongside Jesus. They are all drawn into the drama of the central character whose fate towers over the whole climb. As you read this story, there will almost certainly be someone you can identify with, someone you can come alongside as we make our way up the rock face.

Here, for a start, are several such characters in the opening verses. Each, as it were, is looking up with us at the wall of rock, but from his or her own angle.

Here are the chief priests and elders. For them, the death of Jesus is a political necessity. He has challenged their power, he's captured the crowds' imagination, and he can't be allowed to get away with it. They don't suppose for a minute he might be a true prophet, let alone Israel's Messiah. Their naked political goals, unadorned with any desire for true justice, are a constant feature of the story. Do you know anybody like that? Have you ever seen him or her in the mirror?

Here is a dinner party, the last supper before the Last Supper; and here is an unnamed woman whose love for Jesus has overflowed, quite literally, in an act of needless beauty, like a stunning alpine flower growing unobserved half a mile up a rock face. Of course, some people always want to pick such flowers and make them do something useful – to grow them in a garden at home, perhaps, to make a profit. God's creation isn't like that, and nor is devotion to Jesus. When people start to be captivated by him, and by his path to the cross, the love this produces is given to extravagance. Do you know anybody like that? Does he or she ever wear your shoes?

For Reflection or Discussion

How do you react to the story of Jesus' death? Who do you identify with and why?

WEEK 4: SATURDAY

The Great Commission: Matthew 28.16–20

[16]So the eleven disciples went off to Galilee, to the mountain where Jesus had instructed them to go. [17]There they saw him, and worshipped him, though some hesitated.

[18]Jesus came towards them and addressed them.

'All authority in heaven and on earth', he said, 'has been given to me! [19]So you must go and make all the nations into disciples. Baptize them in the name of the father, and of the son, and of the holy spirit. [20]Teach them to observe everything I have commanded you. And look: I am with you, every single day, to the very end of the age.'

You sometimes wonder, when listening to some of the great classical composers, whether they really know how to bring a piece to an end.

One of the most notorious is Beethoven. There are times when, at the end of a symphony, you think you're just coming to the end, but the chords go crashing on and on, sounding almost 'final' but leaving room for just one more . . . and then another . . . and then another . . . until the very last one dies away and the symphony is truly complete. No doubt a serious student of music would explain that there was a purpose in it, but for many listeners it seems as though a great deal has been packed into the ending, almost as though the whole symphony is being gathered up into those last few explosive chords.

Matthew's ending is much like that. Not that it goes on longer than we expect; it is in fact quite compact. But it contains so much that we would do well to slow down in our reading of these final verses and ponder each line, indeed each phrase, to see how they gather up the whole gospel and pack it tight into the final meeting between Jesus and his followers.

The scene begins on a mountain. No surprises there: a great deal in Matthew happens on a mountain. The temptations; the Sermon on the Mount; the transfiguration; the final discourse on the Mount of Olives; and now this parting scene. Moses and Elijah met the living God on a mountain, and they have appeared in this gospel talking with Jesus; now Jesus invites his disciples to meet him, so that they can be commissioned in turn.

What does surprise us is that, according to Matthew, some of them hesitated. The word can actually mean 'doubt', though we can't be sure how much of that Matthew means here. Did they hesitate over, or doubt, whether it was truly Jesus? Or did they hesitate over, or doubt, whether they, as good Jewish monotheists, believing in YHWH as the one true God, should actually *worship* Jesus? It isn't clear.

What is clear is that the majority of them did worship Jesus, and that Matthew firmly believes this was the right reaction. On several previous occasions in the gospel he has used this word ('worship') to describe people coming reverently to Jesus. Usually it seems to mean simply that they prostrated themselves before him, adopting an attitude of reverence though not necessarily implying that they thought he was divine. (See 8.2; 9.18; 14.33; 15.25; 20.20; and indeed 28.9.) Now, however, to jump for a moment to the last line of the book, it is clear that Matthew wants us to see that in Jesus the promise of the very first chapter has been fulfilled. Jesus is the 'Emmanuel', the one in whom 'God is with us' (1.23). Now he declares that he himself is 'with you always'. The only appropriate reaction to this is indeed worship, worship of the one true God who is now, astonishingly, revealed in and as Jesus himself.

In particular, Jesus has now been given 'all authority in heaven and earth'. In Matthew's account of the temptations the devil offered Jesus this prestige, but without exacting the price that he has now paid (4.8–10). That would have been a hollow triumph, leading to the worst tyranny imaginable. Jesus' authority as the risen one, by contrast, is the authority of the one who has defeated tyranny itself, the ultimate tyranny of death; his is the authority under which life, God's new life, can begin to flourish. Despite what many people today suppose, it is basic to the most elementary New Testament faith that Jesus is *already* ruling the whole world. That is one of the most important results of his resurrection; it is part of the meaning of messiahship, which his new life after the crucifixion has made plain.

People get very puzzled by the claim that Jesus is already ruling the world, until they see what is in fact being said. The claim is not that the world is already completely as Jesus intends it to be. The claim is that he is working to take it from where it was – under the rule not only of death but of corruption, greed and every kind of wickedness – and to bring it, by slow means and quick, under the rule of his life-giving love. And how is he doing this? Here is the shock: *through us, his followers.* The project only goes forward insofar as Jesus' agents, the people he has commissioned, are taking it forward.

Many today mock this claim just as much as they mock the resurrection itself. The church in its various forms has got so much wrong, has made so many mistakes, has let its Lord down so often, that many people, including many who love Jesus for themselves, despair of it and suppose that nothing will ever change until Jesus himself returns to sort it all out. But that isn't Matthew's belief, and it doesn't fit with what we know of Jesus' commissioning of his followers in Luke, Acts and John. It doesn't fit with Paul's vision of his task. They all agree with Matthew: those who believe in Jesus, who are witnesses to his resurrection, are given the responsibility to go and make real in the world the authority which he already has. This, after all, is part of the answer to the prayer that God's kingdom will come on earth as in heaven. If we pray that prayer, we shouldn't be surprised if we are called upon to help bring about God's answer to it.

And so, from the height of this final mountain we look out at God's future from Jesus' perspective, and we see that the 'age to come' has already broken into the 'present age'. This gives us the hope and the confidence that there will

119

come a time when God's will is done on earth as in heaven, because heaven and earth have been joined together in the new creation; when God's kingdom, established by Jesus in his death and resurrection, has finally conquered all its enemies by the power of the divine love; and when, in line with the ancient hopes of Israel, and now with the central intention of Jesus himself, the name of God is honoured, hallowed, exalted and celebrated throughout the whole creation. Every time we say the words 'Our father . . .' we are pleading for that day to be soon, and pledging ourselves to work, in faith, hope and love, to bring it closer.

For Reflection or Discussion

✳ What is your understanding of the claim that Jesus is already ruling the world? How do you react to the daily challenge to bring about God's kingdom?